TRUTH
UNDER
FIRE

TRUTH UNDER FIRE

A Call to Christian Thought
and Action in All of Life

JOHN W. WHITEHEAD

CROSSWAY BOOKS • WHEATON, ILLINOIS
A DIVISION OF GOOD NEWS PUBLISHERS

Truth Under Fire

Copyright © 1998 by John W. Whitehead

Published by Crossway Books
     A division of Good News Publishers
     1300 Crescent Street
     Wheaton, Illinois 60187

First printing, 1998

Printed in the United States of America

ISBN 1-58134-009-5

Library of Congress Cataloging-in-Publication Data

Whitehead, John W., 1946–
    Truth under fire : a call to Christian thought and action in all of life / John W. Whitehead
       p.   cm.
    Includes bibliographical references.
    ISBN 1-58134-009-5
    1. Church and state—United States.   2. Freedom of religion—United States.   3. Christianity and culture—United States.
4. Civil rights—United States.   5. Civil rights—Religious aspects—Christianity.   6. United States—Moral conditions.   7. United States—Religion—1960-   8. United States—History—Religious aspects-Christianity.   I. Title.
BR516.W443 1998
261'.0973—dc21   98-17097

11	10	09	08	07	06	05	04	03	02	01	00	99	98
15	14	13	12	11	10	9	8	7	6	5	4	3	2	1

CONTENTS

HOW DID WE
GET HERE?

> If I profess with the loudest voice and the clearest exposition every portion of the truth of God, except precisely that little point which the world and the devil are at the moment attacking, I am not confessing Christ, no matter how boldly I may be professing Christ.
>
> —MARTIN LUTHER

When we look today at any field of human endeavor, from science to the performing arts, we find scant Christian influence. Indeed, in many areas of life it is as if the Christian worldview never existed.

This is astounding when one realizes it was Judeo-Christian theism that established the philosophical foundations of Western culture and democracy. Without Judeo-Christian presuppositions and principles, it is unlikely that the modern concept of life and freedom would ever have developed.

However, in the modern arts, science, education, law, and government, Judeo-Christian thought no longer plays the leading role. And where its influence is revealed, contemporary society often reacts with contempt. As a result, where Judeo-Christian thought was once predominant, it is now largely only a vestige.

THE SHIFT

Various factors have led to this significant shift in worldview. These, along with an inadequate response by those who espoused Judeo-Christian ideals, have brought modern society to the precipice of nonbelief.

The first factor, modern science, as it was redefined to exclude any concept of a Creator or purposeful design, became not just secularistic but also a potent secularizing force. Far from the science practiced by Newton, Pascal, and others, modern science and the so-called "death of God" movement actually walk hand in hand. As Lucien Goldman notes in *Le Dieu Cache*, the death of God phenomenon is "related to the most important scientific conquest of the age, the discovery of infinite geometric space, and counterposes the silence of God to it. God does not speak any more in the space of rational science because, in order to elaborate the space, man had to renounce every ethical norm." In fact, God is no longer allowed to speak in science because modern science has, by definition, excluded the possibility of divine intervention into a universe rigorously governed by natural laws.

Next, certain philosophical theories have had a great impact, first on major societal institutions and, second, on the general populace. Friedrich Nietzsche, Karl Marx, Sigmund Freud, Charles Darwin, and other thinkers disputed the foundational tenets of Judeo-Christian theism.

Nietzsche's thinking, for example, stridently repudiated Christianity. He argued against the Christian standard of love and the concept that every human being deserves respect. Nietzsche's arguments, some of which have been misinterpreted, have been used to assert that the "super man" or super humans should rule over inferior ones. This philosophy was later reflected in Nazism.

Marx argued for the transformation of human life and nature. He tacitly claimed an egalitarian super status for the mass proletariat. This super status was to be reflected in the state. Communist states and other authoritarian regimes adopted Marx's ideas.

Freud repudiated the Christian concept of sin and theorized that all human disorders are scientifically explicable and capable of cure through therapy. Glenn Tinder commented in an essay "Can We Be Good Without God?" that "The soul was thus severed from God (for Freud, a childish illusion) and placed in the province of human understanding and action."

Finally, the widespread acceptance of Darwin's theory of evolution, as undergirded by modern science, gave a totality to the secular picture of the world. By the time of Darwin's *Origin of Species* in 1859, Christianity had virtually stopped speaking to science. As a consequence, Darwin's theory took the world by storm, and Christianity made no effective response to the evolutionary concept that everything is the product of impersonal agents. From there, it was easy to posit the silence and nonexistence of God.

However, if God is silent, so is all that formerly had spoken loudly of the human being's stature—that is, a person's worth and dignity as he or she stood in the universe. Logically, beings originating from an impersonal source are merely another part of the machinations of "nature"; that is, people are merely products of natural laws—without divine purpose, souls, or a sense of exaltedness.

Governments aligned with this view have been or become, in essence, antihuman. This may be seen in the cruelty of the Chinese government. Human beings are considered mere specks in the universe, something to manipulate or destroy as may be deemed necessary by the state.

COMPARTMENTALIZED
CHRISTIANITY

The net result of the flood of these new ideas, with science at its back, was the compartmentalization of religion and the real world. Thus, there was a gradual move from a total Christianity to a fragmented, compartmentalized religion—from Christianity that urged Christ's lordship in all areas of life to a Christianity that urged a faith based only upon the idealism of the day.

Under the impact of total Christianity, Christians reached out to the culture, not only in personal evangelism but also in science, law, government, education, and the arts. For example, as New York University Professor Neil Postman notes in his book, *Amusing Ourselves to Death,* "the churches in America laid the foundation of our system of higher education." From this era came great educational institutions like Harvard and Yale. Both were established for the combined study of the classics and Christian theology.

Before the twentieth century, most inhabitants of Western society operated on the same presuppositions, which in practice appeared to be in accord with the basic presuppositions of Judeo-Christian theism. Not everyone was a Christian in the true sense of the word. But before 1900, non-Christians nonetheless generally acted on Christian presuppositions.

The basic assumption, still intact in 1900, was that moral absolutes existed. Since moral absolutes can emanate only from an absolute source, it was generally accepted, then, that there was a Supreme Being who dictated a moral system in which life was to be lived. This meant that before 1900 it was still possible to discuss right and wrong (or truth and falsity) with the person on the street.

This all changed beginning in the early years of the twentieth century. The consensus upon which Western culture was built began to shift from one based upon Judeo-Christian theistic principles to a consensus growing out of the Enlightenment.

In the words of Robert Pirsig's modern classic, *Zen and the Art of Motorcycle Maintenance*, "What is good . . . and what is not good—need we ask anyone to tell us these things?"

It is unfortunate that the Christian leaders of the early twentieth century did not effectively challenge the presuppositions of impersonalism before secularism was locked in place. Had they done this, Christians would not have been taken by surprise. Many Christians today have little idea of what occurred or how we got where we are. This is because they are still being taught a one-dimensional view of Christianity.

AFFECTING CULTURE

Too many Christians are passive because they have absorbed decades of teaching that defines Christianity only as a *personal religious experience*. This is a limited, one-dimensional view. This one-dimensional view of Christianity is not enough to discredit impersonalism.

Full-dimensional Christianity, as the apostles taught, means *acting*, from the point of salvation onward, upon the assumption that Christianity is *the* truth. It means affecting culture—the whole spectrum of life.

I must make clear at this point that I am not advocating that any particular religious faith, including Christianity, should subjugate society. However, history does teach that if a total and authentic Christianity is practiced, it will have a substantial positive impact on culture.

Moreover, if the truth of Christianity is in fact *the* Truth, then it stands in antithesis to the ideas and immorality of our age. *This means it must be practiced in the real world, both in teaching and in practical action.*

Truth, however, demands *confrontation*. It must be loving confrontation, but confrontation nonetheless.

It is at this point that many modern Christians, as they quietly live their lives, fall short. And they fall short for two reasons. One is a false view of Christ, and the other is the preference of many modern Christians for accommodation.

Modern Christianity poses Christ in art, speech, and writing as a meek friend of the world. Yet this is not the picture of Him painted by the Gospels. Nor does Christ, the avenger of the book of Revelation, fit this image. And, as John R. W. Stott makes clear in *Christ the Controversialist*, Christ, far from being passive and meek, was controversial and dogmatic.

Jesus Christ was controversial. Stott explains:

> Perhaps the best way to insist that controversy is sometimes a painful necessity is to remember that our Lord Jesus Christ Himself was a controversialist. He was not "broad-minded" in the popular sense that He was prepared to countenance any views on any subject. On the contrary . . . He engaged in continuous debate with the religious leaders of His day, the scribes and Pharisees, the Herodians and Sadducees. He said that He was the truth, that He had come to bear witness to the truth, and that the truth would set His followers free. As a result of His loyalty to the truth, He was not afraid to dissent publicly from official doctrines (if He knew them to be wrong), to expose error, and to warn His disciples of false teachers. He was also extremely outspoken in His language, calling them "blind guides," "wolves in sheep's clothing," "whitewashed tombs" and even a "brood of vipers."

Following Christ's example, the apostles also were controversialists, as is plain from the New Testament Epistles, and they appealed to their readers "to contend for the faith which was once for all delivered to the saints." Like their Lord and Master, they found it necessary to warn the churches of false teachers and to urge them to stand firm in the truth.

Authentic Christianity then, is, by definition, dogmatic. Stott adds:

> We must reply that historic Christianity is essentially dogmatic, because it purports to be a revealed faith. If the Christian religion were just a collection of the philosophical and ethical ideas of men (like Hinduism), dogmatism would be entirely out of place. But if God has spoken (as Christians claim), both in olden days through the prophets and in these last days through His Son, why should it be thought "dogmatic" to believe His Word ourselves and to urge other people to believe it too?

Because many fail to understand the real nature of true Christianity, modern Christians often have a dislike for dogmatism and a hatred for controversy. Thus, modern Christianity has sought to accommodate itself to the thinking of the age.

The secular world, as a whole, does not accommodate authentic Christianity. It will, however, tolerate an accommodating Judaism or Christianity.

Clearly, accommodation has a denigrating effect on the Christian psyche. Seeking approval from the world creates a second-class mentality.

Likewise, when secularists do tolerate an accommodating Christianity, it creates a zookeeper/animal mentality in the Christian. Caged in a secular world, the accommodating Christian becomes fragmented and docile, shying away from controversy. In the next step, very much like zoo animals, Christians begin viewing the secularist-zookeeper as their "friendly" leader.

TRUE
CHRISTIANITY

Through the media of television and radio, modern Christianity has spoken its message to more people more times than ever before in history. Nonetheless, there appears to be a lack of substance behind the basic beliefs held by the average Christian. This is, in part, explained by the lack of rigorous intellectual substance taught from the pulpit and by modern evangelical leaders.

With the rise of a false pietism that came to dominate the churches of the mid-to-late nineteenth century, Christendom, as we have seen, surrendered the *intellectual* front to nonbelievers. This has continued to the present day.

For example, in terms of their intellectual content, the purveyors of modern television Christianity are seriously lacking in substance. As Professor Postman notes, evangelical leaders today often "do not compare favorably with well-known evangelicals of an earlier period, such as Jonathan Edwards, George Whitefield, and Charles Finney, who were men of great learning, theological subtlety, and powerful expositional skills."

These men widely influenced life in Europe and North America. For example, John Nelson Darby and William Kelly developed the theology of dispensationalism and are considered by some to be the originators of what is now called "fundamentalism." J. Gresham Machen argued the Reformed faith from an intellectual standpoint and won the respect of the secularists of his day. Yet these men were persons of enormous erudition, among the most learned of their time. As Professor Postman writes: "In the eighteenth and nineteenth centuries, religious thought and institutions in America were dominated by an austere, learned, and intellectual form of discourse that is largely absent from religious life today."

What the early church, the Reformers, and those mentioned above understood was that Christianity speaks to *all* of life: science, philosophy, art, politics, medicine, and so on. Their view of life was comprehensive, and, for them, *all* truth was God's truth.

For the most part, religious intellectual rigor has declined to the point that much of contemporary Christianity can even be characterized as anti-intellectual. The comprehensive view of life and truth has all but disappeared and has been replaced by a highly compartmentalized and fragmented view that keeps certain disciplines and areas of inquiry off-limits, often because they are considered "worldly."

The fault does not lie entirely with the local church. Modern culture is also highly anti-intellectual, sentimental, and, of course, secularized. The local church, however, has not provided a bulwark against these trends. As observed by Harry Blamires in *The Christian Mind*, it is unfortunate that "the Christian mind has succumbed to the secular drift with a degree of weakness and nervelessness unmatched in Christian history."

An example of contemporary anti-intellectualism is that ministers are often encouraged to "dumb down" their sermons, rather than present more intellectually challenging material. Such sermons often aim at everyone in general and hence speak to no one in particular.

Above all, it is often said that one must "preach a simple Gospel," but this common formulation is misleading. One may preach the Gospel simply, but no Christian, if he or she is faithful to the truths of the Bible, preaches a "simple" Gospel if this means being simplistic.

The Gospel is the eternal God's revelation of Himself in human form and in human history. It is an absolutely stupendous historical event that touches all areas of life and raises countless questions, most of them quite complex. To the extent possible, the Christian should be capable of providing honest and informed answers. Slogans and clichés will not do the job.

This is not an apology for a dry intellectualism, a highbrow or snobbish posture, or for a view that sees the Bible and what it has to say only in terms of ideas. Neither is it a denial of the role of the Holy Spirit in conversion and the Christian life. Rather, it is simply a recognition that a gospel that fails to grapple with all of life is a false gospel, certain to fail in view of the present strong secular opposition, and far removed from what was once characteristic of the Christian church. In simple terms, the contemporary church has lost its intellect and, therefore, its mind.

SPEAKING
TO REAL LIFE

Modern evangelicals have forgotten that one reason Christianity spread was because of its effect on *real* people in dealing with *real* problems in a *real* world. Historic Christianity saw life in its totality, not in fragments. It was a total worldview. There is no longer such a consensus among Christians.

As a thinking being, the modern Christian has succumbed to secularization. He accepts religion—its morality, its worship, its spiritual culture. However, he rejects the total view of life, which sees all earthly issues within the context of the eternal—which relates all human problems—social, political, and cultural—to the doctrinal foundations of the Christian faith. As a consequence, the faith fails to raise the ethical standards of the American population even minimally.

If Christians are to be effective in the face of secularistic depersonalization, they must go through a period of systematic study, thought, and reevaluation that will take much time and energy. Even as this takes place, the forces of depersonalization will increase, for there is little to abate the movement.

It is not that the foundation of truth has changed or that the basic doctrines have lost their meaning but that these need to be expressed and formulated in ways that address the crises of the modern age.

One may study the present situation and point to the fact that the culture seems to be collapsing, notwithstanding its technical achievements and great knowledge in many fields. However, one should not think that this may be attributed only to nonbelievers. It must be realized that Christians are also responsible.

Much of society's condemnation of modern Christians is justified. Why didn't Christians protest long ago? Why weren't they helping the oppressed and poor? Why weren't they reaching out to AIDS victims and sharing the love of Christ? Why did it take the wholesale slaughter of unborn children to bring Christians to their feet? Why aren't Christians evaluating and protesting a secular science rushing headlong toward obliterating human beings as we know them?

True Christianity, I must emphasize again and again, speaks to all of life. It has something to say to all the disciplines. Christianity also has something to say about the problems of our times: the problems of the faceless, mass man, of materialistic technology, of secularism squeezing out human dignity, of the lack of a true foundation for culture.

Christianity, then, expresses a profound realism about the world in which we live. The Bible is very realistic about sorrow, pain, evil, hatred, jealousy, cruelty, and human misery. But the Bible also makes it clear that this is all man's responsibility. It is because of willful human acts against the Creator.

However, true Christianity also *explains* man. Modern secularists do not understand human beings simply because they have no standard, except subjective relativism, by which to explain them. The Fall and the resulting abnormality in humans explains why pain and suffering exist and why people bring curse upon curse upon themselves.

If God appears to withdraw and let people go their own way,

this should cause us to shudder: for the God who hides Himself is also the God who will judge. However, in this way, God shows His intense interest in the worth and dignity of people.

DECLARING
CHRIST

Declaring Christ, as Martin Luther pointedly asserted, is not a simple proposition. In the Christian community, however, it often seems almost painless. Within the confines of our homes, local churches, and Christian business associations, declaring Christ is routine, totally expected. In our daily conversations with other Christians, we often declare Christ repeatedly as we recount prayer requests and praises. We begin our meals and close our meetings with prayer. We broadcast the message of the Gospel across the airwaves to an almost exclusively Christian audience.

But, according to Luther, if this daily routine is our only declaration, we aren't declaring Christ at all. We are only telling what we already know to each other.

So how can we truly declare Christ to the world? We must begin by recognizing the extent of our society's need for Christ. The early church and the Reformers, including Luther, understood the lordship of Christ. Yet this comprehensive view of life has all but disappeared in the mire of compartmentalization.

Our fragmented outlook is most poignantly demonstrated in the area of the arts. In the past century, Christians have, with minimal success, embraced political discourse, engaged scientific discussion, and opened philosophical debate, while practically ignoring the arts. When Christians do pay attention, it is usually to criticize or boycott a particular artist or film. But effective creative expression by Christians is practically nonexistent in the present day.

Contrast this present reality with the Renaissance or

Reformation. It is no coincidence that the impassioned cultural engagement of Christian leaders like Luther coincided with some of the greatest religious art the world has ever seen. Biblical images such as Dierick Bouts' *Virgin and Child* and Rembrandt's *The Shepherds Worship the Child* dominated the visual arts. These talented artists confronted their world with a unique declaration of Christ.

The traditional, historical view of Christianity held that the arts, human creativity, and the beauty of the creation are gifts from God and need no justification on spiritual or utilitarian grounds. They are valuable in themselves and were put here for our enjoyment.

Modern Christianity, however, has largely lost this truth. One would be hard-pressed to find leading artists today who are true believers. The same could be said for aesthetics in general. While Picasso is a household name and millions file into the theaters to watch films by Steven Spielberg and other popular filmmakers, many Christians languish in a subculture devoid of any recognized creativity. Art is the antenna of culture; yet too many Christians have ceased to pay attention.

To declare Christ truly, Christians must climb out of their cultural catacombs and engage the culture. At first, this will be difficult. Just as the Christian community shares a common dialect, which is incomprehensible at times to nonbelievers, the arts and culture speak a common language that the Christian community often misunderstands. Yet if we are to declare Christ to our society, we must speak its language. We must become culturally literate in the broadest sense, while remembering that fluency in cultural endeavors does not require us to adopt the beliefs and moral outlook they embody.

We can take as our model those missionaries who venture into uncharted territories to declare Christ to unreached peoples. Missionaries in this situation must often observe the culture for many years before they can begin their ministry. They patiently watch, recognizing that preaching the Gospel outside of the cultural context of their audience is ultimately fruitless.

The results of declaring Christ authentically could restructure the world as we know it. A reassertion of the Judeo-Christian ethic in the arts, for instance, could very well trickle down throughout society. Again, the influence of film, painting, television, and other creative endeavors is breathtaking. Sadly, few, if any, Christians are significantly involved in any of these areas.

An authentic declaration of the lordship of Christ will require us to continue declaring Him in our homes, churches, and business associations. But we must also begin to declare Him in all those areas that have been largely neglected in this century.

TRUE
FREEDOM

AN
AMERICAN DREAM

When we celebrate the birth of our country on the Fourth of July, it's a good time to step back and consider America's future. Will our society continue to prosper? Or will it, like overripe fruit, burst from its own indulgence?

Like many, I'm concerned that the latter may be true. America may turn out to be a historical accident—a brief parenthesis that is closing before our eyes. This can be seen in the numerous end-time scenarios that pervade our culture, including the mass suicide of the Heaven's Gate cult.

Paul Simon aptly summed up this mood in his song "American Tune":

> I don't know a soul who's not been battered
> I don't have a friend who feels at ease
> I don't know a dream that's not been shattered
>   or driven to its knees
> But it's all right, it's all right
> We've lived so well so long
> Still, when I think of the road
>   we're traveling on
> I wonder what went wrong
> I can't help it, I wonder what went wrong.

These lyrics, written at the height of the Watergate scandal of the early 1970s, more accurately portray the mood of America now than when they were written. The "Age of Aquarius" did not follow on the heels of the 1960s. Instead of the dawning of a new age, frustration and alienation followed. Next came the apathy and smug materialism of the eighties and the endless search for meaning of the nineties. The hope for a new beginning has been lost.

America began with a dream. This dream, the American dream, is what has made the rest of the world look to America in hope. All too often, the American dream is now defined in material terms—a new house, a well-paying job, and two cars in the driveway. But to the nation's founders, the American dream was much more.

The Declaration of Independence and the history that preceded it are where we must look to find what has come to be called the American dream. In it, we find three fundamental concepts: rights, resistance, and optimism about the future. These three themes run throughout the history of this country. Their current demise is peculiar to modern-day America.

Civil liberties, especially those of religious persons, are violated by government entities on a daily basis.

Resistance, or at least intelligent resistance, is practically nonexistent. Those who adapt the mantle of resistance in our times can only articulate a violent response—a far cry from the reasoned intelligence of our Founding Fathers.

As for future optimism, many are looking forward to a bright economic future. However, the moral core of our culture is in decline, and no one seems to have a legitimate solution.

Thomas Jefferson, who penned the Declaration, told James Madison in an 1823 letter that he meant the document to be "an expression of the American mind, and to give to that expression the proper tone and spirit called for by the occasion."

If there is to be any real freedom for all and optimism for the future, we must recover the ideals that are set forth in the Declaration of Independence.

Our task is to attempt such a recovery. If not, the American tune may soon be only a faint whisper in a storm of despair.

THE POINT IS . . .

"We hold these truths to be self-evident, that all men are created equal, that they are endowed by their Creator with certain unalienable Rights, that among these are Life, Liberty, and the pursuit of Happiness. That to secure these rights, Governments are instituted among Men, deriving their just powers from the consent of the governed; that whenever any Form of Government becomes destructive of these ends, it is the Right of the People to alter or abolish it, and to institute new Government."

These are the opening lines of the Preamble to the Declaration of Independence. In the years following its drafting, this Preamble was translated into the basic institutions of the American republic. Yet what has become of the ideals set forth in the Declaration of Independence over the last two hundred years? Like a ship drifting out to sea, these ideals are slowly fading.

The point is that we must not lose the heritage of religious and other freedoms in America. When you celebrate the Fourth of July, I encourage you to do your part to preserve religious freedom. Take the time to learn the history of religious freedom in America.

A CONSERVATIVE SUPREME COURT?

The United States Supreme Court spent the third week of June 1997 issuing several of its most significant rulings for the decade. In just two days, free exercise protections for millions of religious Americans were stricken from federal law, pornographic images were left to proliferate in the wilds of the Internet jungle without legal interference, and states were told to decide for themselves whether or not they wanted to let their residents end their lives with the aid of a doctor. It is now apparent that twelve years of conservative presidents did nothing to change the judiciary's "progressive" course.

In 1980, conservatives heralded the election of Ronald Reagan as the dawn of a new era. Popular wisdom predicted that Reagan would appoint conservative justices, and soon the tide of liberal decisions would begin to turn. In 1984, the people reelected Reagan, and conservatives swelled with confidence. In 1988, George Bush continued the run with his victory over Michael Dukakis. Any remaining doubts vanished—the 1990s would definitely herald a new beginning for the judiciary. Led by the Supreme Court of Reagan and Bush, the courts surely would deliver a string of decisions reasserting the rights of religious persons in America's public arena and respect under the law for the value of human life.

It could have happened. As of June 1997, five of the nine justices were appointed by either Reagan or Bush—a clear majority. The revolution, however, did not materialize. And the Supreme Court's June 1997 decisions only confirmed a growing suspicion: these justices are not allies of religious persons. In fact, this Court has actually provided new rationales for excluding religion and religious belief from public life.

For example:

Justice Anthony Kennedy, a Reagan appointee, held in *Lee v. Weisman* (1992) that school-sponsored graduation prayer is unconstitutional in public schools and asserted that religion belongs in what he termed the "private sphere."

Justice Antonin Scalia, another Reagan pick, is widely considered to be the most conservative member of the Supreme Court. Yet in *Employment Division v. Smith* (1990), he said that freedom of religion is secondary to other rights.

Justice Kennedy was joined by fellow Reagan appointee Sandra Day O'Connor and Bush appointee David Souter in the plurality opinion when the Supreme Court reaffirmed the right to abortion with its ruling in *Planned Parenthood v. Casey* (1992).

Then, in June 1997, the Reagan/Bush legacy struck down the Religious Freedom Restoration Act (RFRA). By a 6-3 vote, the Court ruled Congress had overstepped its bounds in its attempt to protect religious individuals and groups from laws that seem neutral on the surface but actually have the effect of infringing on religious freedom.

Congress enacted RFRA to restore traditional free exercise of religion rights that were swamped in the wake of *Smith*. Led by Justice Scalia's majority decision, the Supreme Court ruled in *Smith* that religious persons are not exempt from laws that are neutral "on their face"—even if obeying the law violates a deeply-held religious belief.

The Rutherford Institute has used RFRA to help churches fight zoning laws that constricted their ministry, assist Amish hunters in their attempts to opt out of state laws requiring orange clothing, and acquire religious magazines for a Virginia death row inmate.

But the Court didn't stop with religious individuals and groups. Next, they turned their sights on the critically ill. At first glance, the June 26 decision to uphold bans on assisted suicide in Washington and New York seems laudable. But closer scrutiny reveals its implications are more ominous.

Although the nine justices were unanimous in their decision, various concurring opinions illustrate that the issue is far from settled. For instance, Justice Stevens wrote that while Washington State's prohibition on assisted suicide was not invalid on its face, the Court's decision "did not foreclose the possibility that some applications of the statute might well be invalid."

In addition, the ruling left the door open for states to pass laws that specifically *permit* assisted suicide. Oregon already has such a statute, and other states may soon follow.

The underlying message in this labyrinth of decisions and opinions is clear: the Supreme Court cannot revive American society. It will not lead religious people, unborn children, and concerned parents into a bright new millennium. It will not fulfill any "conservative" dream.

So where do religious Americans turn? For now the burden falls on grassroots organizations battling at the lowest levels of the court system for the rights of individual citizens. Groups like The Rutherford Institute will bear the brunt of an ever-increasing workload. As the caseload grows, however, the list of legal options is shrinking.

This will require the efforts of more attorneys, most of whom donate their time for free. It will require funds from grants and caring individuals to cover legal expenses. It will require the courage of students, parents, employees, churches, and anyone else who faces religious discrimination to stand up for their rights. It will not be easy.

THE POINT IS . . .

Have you ever looked to a political leader to save America from her moral decay? Or have you placed your faith in a political party or ideology? These days, with the resurgence of Christians in politics, it's easy to look to charismatic men and women for the answers to our nation's problems—especially when they happen to be Christians. But, as the psalmist warns us, we must not put our "trust in princes, in mortal men, who cannot save us."

Still, this doesn't mean that Christians are to avoid the political arena entirely. In fact, Christians are called to be involved in their society—to be salt and light. So as you walk the delicate tightrope between politics and religion, here are some principles to help you keep your balance.

One. Don't sacrifice your religious beliefs to advance a political agenda. Remember, the purpose of Christian political involvement is to speak the truth and, it is hoped, have a positive effect on the political process. Two. Be aware of your own fallibility. Humility, not extremism, should characterize the Christian. Three. Resist the temptation to solve spiritual problems through exclusively political means. The real duty of Christians is to proclaim and live out the Gospel of Jesus Christ.

The point is that the true Christian is one who thinks deeply, prays fervently, and acts lovingly. Abiding by these standards, Christians can have political influence and preserve their witness.

WHEN FREE SPEECH AND MORALITY COLLIDE— AN AMERICAN PREDICAMENT

When I read about the most recent free speech controversy, I sometimes feel that Americans have walked into a predicament. On the one hand, we claim that everyone has the right to freedom of expression. On the other, we try to impose some sort of morality on free speech, even though we do not agree what this morality should be.

As a result of this contradiction, we find strange inconsistencies in the application of our First Amendment rights. For example, it may be okay to publish certain pornographic materials but not okay to sexually harass a coworker. Shouting "FIRE" in a crowded theater or making discriminatory jokes is likewise out of line, but lying about a public religious figure in a "parody" may be permitted. Some judgments we welcome. Others give rise to continued controversy.

For example, Paladin Press was recently sued for publishing a how-to-murder manual. The book was allegedly used by a hit man to kill two women and a quadriplegic eight-year-old boy. The book contained explicit directions for the most efficient murder weapons and how to use them. Should Paladin be held accountable for aiding the crime?

That's a hard question to answer because we live in a conflicted society. We all want our own freedom—and we fear that if we try to crack down on someone else, we'll suffer, too. In the Paladin case, many newspapers and publishers joined the side of Paladin Press, claiming that the lawsuit would have a chilling effect on free speech.

I believe this controversy serves to show just how far we've strayed from the principles upon which our country was founded. When our Founding Fathers wrote the Constitution, questions like this were hardly a serious concern. They lived in a society where most people would not have produced, published, or purchased anything like a murder manual. To put it bluntly, many Americans had an internal morality, based on Judeo-Christian ethics, which constrained them from "expressing themselves" to the detriment of others. And, in a society like this, free speech could flourish—because people governed themselves.

Today, unfortunately, many Americans seem to have fewer qualms about doing harm to others. And the same Constitution that was designed to protect our society when most people were subject to internal moral restraint now protects people who care about nothing more than making a dollar. Because of this shift in morality, we find ourselves trying to defend our own right to free speech by siding with a publisher who may have contributed to a brutal murder. What a predicament.

On a strictly political level, we're faced with a choice between absolute freedom for everybody (anarchy) or absolute governmental control (authoritarianism). But I have some hope that we won't be forced to choose either one. I hope there are still enough thoughtful people who can choose the third option—self-control, personal discipline, and consideration for the well-being of others. I hope these same individuals pass these values on to the next generation. This is the only way to maintain freedom of speech without taking advantage of one another.

The First Amendment was an inspired creation, and free

speech is something we all cherish. But a voluntary shift toward a moral mentality is the only way a free nation can remain free.

THE POINT IS . . .

For decades, visitors to Colonial Williamsburg have stood in long lines to tour the Wythe House. But few tour guides take the time to share the profound influence that this forefather of freedom had on forming our system of government.

In the early days of Williamsburg, a respected resident named George Wythe became a lawyer, judge, and teacher. Among his other stately achievements, Wythe signed the Declaration of Independence and contributed to the drafting of the United States Constitution.

But Wythe's lesser-known contributions to American government were probably his most important—his perspectives on law, liberty, and the separation of powers. Wythe strongly believed that people needed freedom with limits, not license. He promoted a government by law, not anarchy. He believed the colonists' new laws should be built upon the solid foundation of the English Bill of Rights and the Magna Charta. But Wythe also insisted that government needed limits. Today, these limits are the checks and balances system between the branches of federal government—a system, Mr. Wythe knew, that would restrict any one branch from becoming too powerful.

The point is, although George Wythe isn't as famous as his star pupil, Thomas Jefferson, his contribution to the formation of our United States was invaluable. We should never underestimate the importance of one individual. Which reminds me: what have you done to preserve your freedom today?

The Meaning
of Life

DON'T LOOK BACK: TWENTY-FIVE YEARS OF *ROE V. WADE*

> The blood-dimmed tide is loosed, and everywhere
> The ceremony of innocence is drowned.
> —WILLIAM BUTLER YEATS,
> *THE SECOND COMING*

Yeats could just as easily have penned those words when we "celebrated" the twenty-fifth anniversary of *Roe v. Wade*, the Supreme Court decision that loosed the "blood-dimmed tide." On January 22, 1973, the Court decided that Jane Roe did, in fact, have the right to abort her child (even though her child had already been born), and, with that ruling, "things fell apart."

One merely has to scan the daily headlines to see where *Roe* has taken us: an infant girl was found in a toilet at Disney World, her umbilical cord wrapped around her neck; a nineteen-year-old Arizona woman was accused of drowning her newborn and hiding its body in a coffee can; a New York woman was arraigned on murder charges after giving birth on a toilet and letting the infant drown in the bowl; a New Jersey girl gave birth during her prom and left her child to die in the bathroom. And, as columnist George Will points out, these are just the known cases.

Where do these mothers get the idea that it's acceptable to

murder their children? If they don't get it from society's general lack of respect for life (see Oregon's assisted-suicide law; Bill Clinton's veto of the bill banning partial-birth abortions), they can find some rationale in publications by "experts" on the issue. For example, in a *New York Times Magazine* article, MIT psychology professor Steven Pinker writes: "Several moral philosophers have concluded that neonates are not persons, and thus neonaticide should not be classified as murder." This could be read as saying, in other words, that infanticide is acceptable.

But Pinker is apparently not alone. In her book *Unzipped Genes*, Washington lawyer Martine Rothblatt argues that pregnancy is a disease, comparing it to smallpox. Rothblatt argues that all male teenagers should have vasectomies to ensure that no woman is "infected" with unwanted pregnancy. Using Rothblatt's rationale, children from unwanted pregnancies are byproducts of disease—boils to be lanced. Her argument seems to suggest that women who kill their unwanted babies are akin to schoolchildren who scratch their chicken pox—not necessarily a good idea, but really no big deal.

If this, then, is where we have come after twenty-five years, where will the next twenty-five take us? The future looks grim indeed. The pro-life community has warned of the implications of *Roe* ever since 1973. Most of the experts either ignored these warnings or scoffed at them. But today our government ponders whether to endorse human cloning, whether to allow doctors to end their patients' lives, whether killing children who have been partially born is protected under *Roe*, and whether to approve drugs that would make abortion as simple as taking an aspirin. And the government has already approved experiments using human embryos.

Sadly, most Americans don't really care about these issues anymore. They are weary of the full-scale abortion wars that led to legislation such as the Freedom of Access to Clinic Entrances

Act (FACE). Violence at abortion clinics, including the murder of abortion doctors, has frightened the American public from seriously considering the morality of the issue. Many persons today recite the mantra, "I don't believe in it, but let the woman decide." But this *laissez-faire* position ignores the personhood of the fetus—a truth that is acknowledged, at least indirectly, by most physicians.

In *The Second Coming*, Yeats laments, "The best lack all conviction, while the worst/Are full of passionate intensity." This has never been more true than in America today. I would hope that on this twenty-fifth anniversary of the nadir of American society, we would, as a country, reconsider our position. But I doubt this will happen. And I fear for the future.

THE POINT IS . . .

Alabama Circuit Court Judge Randall Thomas stepped down from the bench to step up to a higher call. During his twenty-one years on the bench, Thomas was not free to speak out about his political views: he was constrained by his position as a judge. And that was just fine with him, until one day in the spring of 1997.

Thomas was driving home from the courthouse listening to the radio. The program reported that President Clinton had vetoed legislation banning partial-birth abortions. Though Thomas was pro-life, he really had no idea what partial-birth abortions were. So he asked around. A doctor with a crisis pregnancy center described the horrifying procedure to him. The image of partial-birth abortions was forever etched in his mind. Judge or not, Thomas knew he could no longer remain silent. He had a mission from God: "to educate people about, and denounce, partial-birth abortions."

The point is that this judge willingly stepped down from his bench to follow a higher call. He gave up being a justice in order to execute justice for the speechless and for the unborn. You may not need to give up your job for the unborn. You may simply need to open your home to a pregnant teen, or volunteer at a local crisis pregnancy center, or cast your ballot for those who protect life. Just be sure you do something to speak up for those who can't yet speak and who, because of abortion, never will.

OF FATE AND HEADLESS FROGS

The scientists have done it again. After the earth-shaking revelation that the Scots had cloned a sheep, British scientists in London reported that they had created a frog embryo without a head.

Far from going unnoticed, the announcement set off another storm of controversy, primarily because this breakthrough may open doors for cloning human organs without the rest of the body. Someone who needed a liver transplant, for example, could clone another human being with the same genetic composition—only instead of having a complete body, they'd just grow a new liver and repress the growth of other, unnecessary organs. Soon, scientists could have laboratories throbbing with artificial wombs sheltering hearts, kidneys, and livers awaiting harvest.

At first, this appears to be a solution to a genuine medical dilemma. According to some reports, seven to nine persons die nationwide each day while waiting for an organ transplant. A new individual is added to the organ waiting list every eighteen minutes—a list that includes approximately 55,000 people in the United States. With over 7,000 people waiting just for a donated liver, there simply aren't enough to go around. About one-third of these with heart or liver failure die before they can find a suitable transplant organ, and controversy surrounds who should have priority when transplant organs become available.

In light of all this, a source of unlimited organs might seem to be a light in a dark tunnel, especially to the families of those waiting for an organ donation. They live each day with the fear of losing their loved ones, and who could blame them for seizing on a new chance for life?

Yet the real problem with cloning organs by growing embryos just for that purpose is the question about the value of human beings and what makes them who they are. Scientists and theologians have struggled over this issue for the length of human existence—in debates over the beginning of life, the definition of life, a person's individuality, and the existence of an immortal soul. Depending on an individual's religious or nonreligious orientation, the answers vary. But most honest people would agree, as do many new mothers when they first gaze into their baby's eyes, that a human being is a unique mystery. And all of us, somewhere deep inside, believe we are somehow important in the grand scheme of things.

Growing babies for their organs plays with the very essence of what makes us human. If we choose to grow a whole crop of children simply for harvest, we have determined, somehow, that people with scientific usefulness don't deserve to live. That determination may seem simple enough when the infant is only the size of a few growing cells. But, if we're honest with ourselves, we're probably all scientifically useful in some way. We've just been fortunate enough, so far, to escape the clutches of those who might want to experiment on us or use us as part of their experimentations. We use a double standard when we protect ourselves but discriminate against helpless children.

(Lest this sound far-fetched, consider the horrific experiments conducted on non-Aryan adults in Nazi prison camps. They were exposed to infectious diseases, plunged into sub-zero temperatures so doctors could watch them freeze to death, deprived of oxygen, and subjected to other experiments that also led to agonizing deaths.)

While it is true that cloning organs may be a "workable" solution for heartbreaking issues, what it actually comes down to in the end is whether or not something is "right" just because it is workable. The truth is, if experimentation does deny human dignity, if it does devalue human beings, if it does discriminate between classes of people, we can't afford to choose these options—no matter how many other problems they appear to solve.

In the end, there is no scientific reason not to create children just for harvesting their organs—unless you and I and every human being has value, dignity, and maybe even a soul.

THE POINT IS . . .

When it comes to the debate surrounding the sanctity of human life, abortion is just the tip of the iceberg. Once our nation adopted the abortion mentality of Roe v. Wade, it quickly lost its footing and slipped on steadily more treacherous layers of scientific exploration—the latest of which is known as human cloning.

In a cutting-edge venture, a Houston-based company named Cryogenic Solutions, Inc., is marketing a procedure known as cryopreservation. A CSI brochure explains that a woman having an abortion may ask her doctor to "remove the embryo and suspend its development using cryopreservation" instead of discarding the unwanted fetal tissue. If and when a woman decides she's ready to have a baby, CSI claims it can continue the development of her previously aborted embryo.

But the truth is that the unborn baby no longer exists. What CSI really is doing is preserving cells of an aborted fetus, implanting them in a new egg, and recreating another human being—a process commonly referred to as cloning.

The point is that the race to patent technology to make an unwanted, aborted fetus become a wanted, genetically-engineered baby has begun. The opportunity for financial rewards is enormous, but the penalty for playing God won't be worth it. As this game of life unravels, is the church sitting on the sidelines, or is it a player training for the fight of its life?

WHAT DOES IT MEAN TO BE HUMAN?

In the film *Groundhog Day*, Bill Murray experiences the opportunity of a lifetime: to relive the same day over and over again. At first, he reacts selfishly. Eventually, though, he concludes that he should make the most of his one day to live. Heroically, he attempts to prevent every tragedy that he has foreknowledge of and even performs a few acts of pure kindness. At the end, when he wakes up to discover that time has started to move forward again, the audience sighs with relief, glad that Bill can get on with his life, now that he's gotten things right.

Although it's been a number of years since the film was released, *Groundhog Day* presents an eternal human desire. Especially after a dismal failure, we would all love a chance to repeat the whole thing and "do it right this time."

Unfortunately, though, we can't reenact the past. Unlike Bill Murray, we have to live with the consequences of our poor choices. And, as I look back at some recent events, I am particularly reminded of several "choices" Americans will be living with for a long time: the cloning of a sheep, Supreme Court decisions concerning assisted suicide, and Internet censorship. These events, diverse and seemingly unrelated, touch us at our very core and raise the question—what does it mean to be human?

The bombshell was probably the news that a sheep had been cloned. On top of the advances made in related fields such as genetics and embryology, this breakthrough took us one step further down the road to the creation of made-to-order human beings—and the disposal of them by using their organs for other purposes.

Although many people initially seemed horrified at the prospect, after thinking more about it, human cloning didn't seem so far-fetched after all. According to Lori Andrews, an expert on the legal issues of reproduction, this change in attitude from horror to acceptance was "very, very quick." Simply put, the idea of harvesting human beings no longer bothers many people.

The 1997 Supreme Court ruling that no one has a constitutionally protected right to physician-assisted suicide may also have earthshaking ramifications. Although at first glance this might seem like a victory for life, the ruling left open the distinct possibility that individual states *can* choose to make such suicide legal—as Oregon has already done.

Going along with this, a national Harris Poll reported that 68 percent of respondents agreed a doctor should be able to prescribe a lethal dose of drugs if requested by a terminally-ill person at the end of life. Such decisions and polls leave us looking toward a future where assisted suicide may be the norm rather than the exception. The message? Life is disposable when it becomes inconvenient or painful.

The third issue involves Internet censorship. When the Supreme Court struck down portions of the Communications Decency Act of 1996, it left the Internet open for the transfer of offensive materials, including certain types of pornography. While the ruling was a confirmation of America's right to free speech, it will also dramatically affect the availability and use of questionable materials. It leaves censorship decisions in the hands of individuals, and their choices will affect lives. A whole is the sum of its parts, and American society as a whole will be affected by how individuals view other human beings—as people with dignity or as commodities to be used.

The ramifications of these events may point us toward a grave future where human beings are created to be used, life is valuable only when it is convenient, and people are nothing more than bodies. We don't have the opportunity, like Bill Murray, to start over—and over and over. We will live with the consequences of recent years for a long time to come. On the other hand, we can make a difference in the future, and it may not be too late to see change for the good.

THE POINT IS . . .

It's recycling day. Time to set out the old newspapers and aluminum cans. Unfortunately, aluminum cans and newspapers aren't the only resources being recycled. A far more precious resource, that of unborn human babies, is being recycled.

With the approval of President Bill Clinton, parts of aborted human fetuses are being transplanted into humans with illnesses such as Parkinson's disease. Though politicians, doctors, and the general public prefer to call the procedure fetal transplantation, human recycling is a more accurate description of the practice. To date, brain cells from aborted babies have been recycled in over two hundred people afflicted with Parkinson's disease—and with mixed results, I might add.

The point is that even if diseases could be cured by the injection of parts of aborted fetuses, the practice is morally wrong. Recycling aborted human babies sends a message that it's okay to abort babies because something good comes out of the abortions. To mothers considering an abortion, the possibility that the product of abortions might help another numbs the pain of killing an unborn baby. And it gives the public an excuse to support giving women a choice to terminate their pregnancies. So next time you drag your recycling bin out to the driveway, remember, some things were never meant to be recycled.

MICROMANAGING LIFE

A growing number of Americans are spending more time planning their deaths than their lives. They meet with estate lawyers, insurance agents, and health-care providers to ensure that their passage from life to death is as seamless as possible.

People didn't always spend so much time and energy planning for death. They didn't have time because they were too busy living to worry about dying. Sure, they may have been concerned about death, but it wasn't the most important thing in their lives.

Times have changed. Today, people want to be in charge and in control of everything. They want to maximize their quality of life, minimize their dependence on others, and totally eliminate their risk of pain. They even want to control the ultimately uncontrollable event—death.

Should individuals have the right to control when and how they die? In the summer of 1997, the United States Supreme Court had the opportunity to address this question.

The case before the Supreme Court was *Vacco v. Quill.* The question: Does a New York law that prohibits doctor-assisted suicide violate the Fourteenth Amendment's Equal Protection Clause?

The doctors who filed the lawsuit claimed that it would be "consistent with the standards of [their] medical practice[s]" to prescribe lethal medication for "mentally competent, terminally ill patients" who are suffering great pain and desire a doctor's help in taking their own lives.

They reasoned that since it was legal for a competent patient to refuse life-sustaining medical treatment, it should be similarly permissible for that patient to commit suicide with the help of his physician since the two "treatments" were, in the words of the doctors, "essentially the same thing." The High Court didn't agree.

Rather, in a unanimous ruling, the Supreme Court found a significant difference between a patient refusing life-sustaining treatment and a doctor assisting a patient's suicide through prescribing lethal medication. It was a difference in both cause and intent.

When a patient refuses life-sustaining medical treatment, the cause of his death is an underlying fatal disease. But if a patient ingests lethal medication prescribed by his physician, the cause of his death is that medication. In the case of a patient refusing life-sustaining treatment, the doctor allows the disease to run its course. In the case of physician-assisted suicide, the doctor intends to assist in his patient's death. Such is not the role of a medical doctor.

To protect and preserve life is not only the proper role of the physician but also one of the legitimate roles of the state. In the case of assisted suicide, the government has a recognized interest in protecting those who are not competent to protect their own lives, those who are not actually facing imminent death, and those whose death would not be truly voluntary.

Thus, in deciding *Vacco v. Quill*, the Court found that physician-assisted suicide conflicts with the state's interests in preserving life. Yet the Supreme Court justices didn't completely slam the door on physician-assisted suicide. They left it open a crack by suggesting that, under certain conditions, they might see a constitutional right to die that outweighs the state's interest in preserving life.

For now, there is no constitutional right to die—with or without dignity. But *for now* won't last long.

Unfortunately, we live with a Court that is willing to create new constitutional rights. Certainly if the High Court has given women the right to control their own bodies by killing their unborn babies, we may see the day when it will give individuals the right to control their own bodies by killing themselves at the hands of their physician. If control is what the public wants, then control may be what they get—even if it kills them.

THE POINT IS . . .

Have some high schools and abortion clinics become silent partners? Just take a look at what these "partners" did to Clara Wilker.

When Clara suspected she might be pregnant, she wasn't sure where to turn. So she turned to her high-school guidance counselors in Pittsfield, Massachusetts. The counselors never contacted Clara's parents. Instead, they falsified hall passes for Clara so that they could take her to a Western Massachusetts Family Planning Clinic. And once at the clinic, counselors urged Clara to abort her child.

Fortunately, Clara decided not to go through with the abortion. Unfortunately, she waited over five months to tell her mother about her pregnancy. During this time, the clinic failed to provide her with adequate medical treatment. As a result, Clara now suffers from occasional paralysis and headaches.

On behalf of Clara and her family, The Rutherford Institute filed a lawsuit against Pittsfield High School administrators and guidance counselors, as well as the abortion clinic. The lawsuit alleges they tried to coerce sixteen-year-old Clara Wilker into having an abortion.

The point of law is parental rights. School officials should not have falsified hall passes and removed Clara from school to take her to an abortion clinic. And clinic counselors should not have urged this young woman to abort her baby.

Has your local school teamed up with an abortion clinic? Are school officials escorting students to family planning clinics? You have rights. And by learning about them, you may save the life of someone you love.

Humanity's Search for Meaning: Implications for Religious Liberty

(The following is an excerpt from John Whitehead's speech presented at The Rutherford Institute's International Conference on Religious Liberty in Europe, held in 1997 in Paris.)

What gives us, as human beings, worth and dignity?

The answer to this eternal question is inextricably linked with our struggle to preserve and protect humankind's great liberties, such as freedom of conscience and the right to life itself. The answer is critical to the state as well as the individual believer.

For example, up until the twentieth century, it was generally believed in Western society that men, women, and children possessed an inherent value that could not legitimately be taken away or destroyed by other human beings or governments.

This belief was derived in great part from traditional Judeo-Christian beliefs. As the distinguished French philosopher Henri Bergson (1859-1941) noted, "Humanity had to wait till Christianity for the idea of universal brotherhood, with its implication of equality of rights and the sanctity of the person to become operative."

In the past, Judeo-Christian religious traditions provided a foundation upon which people could base their claims of individual worth and dignity—apart from the support of the state. This is true, even though people have not practiced the Judeo-

Christian religion in anything nearing perfection, as may be seen with the acceptance of slavery. Nonetheless, where Judeo-Christian principles have been applied more or less consistently, such as in many Western nations, a high view of humanity has been fostered and the state has been held accountable, in varying degrees, to a more humanizing view of people.

Religious traditions, whatever their derivation and contour, inevitably forge some link between the individual and the state. Religion, as it is expressed in political systems, provides the normative judgment of where citizens *should* fit. Religion explains the moral significance of social institutions such as the family and also law and education. Religion provides a basis for obedience—or resistance—to what the state accomplishes and what it orders.

Thus, every government must, at one level or another, frame its legitimacy as part of a larger context. Moreover, no state can secure an enduring legitimacy solely through force or a so-called social contract, which is simply an association of individuals who band together out of a mutual self-interest.

The moral, and therefore legitimate, state must provide not only for freedom of conscience but also for the effective and equal political participation of *all* religious faiths so that religious liberty—with all its benefits for the state as well as the individual—may be preserved. This means that no one, whatever his or her beliefs, is to be excluded from society and equal protection under the law. This is the *only* humane way to treat people.

The defining characteristic of much of modern Western culture, however, is its denial of absolute truth—such as the truth of the worth and dignity of each individual person. One result is an unprecedented upheaval in every area of life and the loss of basic truths to live by.

Moreover, much of modern life is characterized by a dehumanized view of people and a bewildered acceptance of conflict and persecution around the world. The atrocities and carnage of the wars of the twentieth century and the continuing oppression of people worldwide are clear examples of this. Extreme cruelty, such as that faced by the Jews in the 1930s and 1940s, has become a hallmark of the twentieth century. Abortion, the demise of the traditional family, state persecution and suppression of religious groups, and a general hopelessness are horrible ills that each and every one of us face—individually and as a nation. Dehumanized, much of modern Western society has been reduced to a collective struggle for survival and the will to overpower other human beings as well as the forces of nature and technology.

As a result, the great quest of modern humanity—for liberty, equality, and brotherhood—has, in many instances, become an illusion, a dream that may no longer be achievable. Even where this slogan is the banner cry, the result is often unspeakable and unrestrained horror, as happened in the French Revolution of the late nineteenth century.

But the people of our modern era still yearn for liberty, equality, and the pursuit of happiness—and for all of the individual worth included in these concepts. Many seek to fill this yearning with various religious perspectives that are often at odds with each other.

In most Western nations, it will be difficult for these various religious perspectives to exist as equals. Too often, the struggle for religious supremacy—perhaps even religious survival—becomes the struggle for political supremacy. This struggle carries with it the right and power to define a culture and determine its worldview, institutions, destiny, and, ultimately, its view of people and how they should be treated.

Thus, the political domination of a culture by any one religious view necessarily implies that the state—at a minimum—ignores the validity of principles and truths held dearly by others—and perhaps even suppresses them. At the extreme, the state may exercise its power to persecute views with which it does not agree.

Given the importance of religious belief to society and the

dangers to a culture of religious domination of the government's power, the question then becomes how to define the appropriate role of religion with respect to the conduct of the affairs of the state. The answer directly implicates essential human rights, such as religious liberty, as well as the stability of the state itself.

The most appropriate role of religion in culture lies in its ability to *define* moral issues and provide the *traditional authority* for their solutions. Religion provides the moral vision—the moral compass—for society.

Whatever its tenets, religion explains the *moral significance* of social institutions such as family and law and, indeed, government itself. Religion provides the *imperative for obedience or resistance* to what the state accomplishes and what it orders. Religion can do this most effectively—and most durably—*apart* from the power of the state. Even an individual believer can, as history illustrates, become the moral conscience of a nation. For example, one person, holding his or her Torah or the Bible, can bring down the tyranny of the state.

The voice of moral authority raised *without* dependence upon legitimization by the state is the highest expression of true religious freedom. Such a voice denies the ultimate authority of the government to create or define right or wrong by its own power. This is certainly the Judeo-Christian heritage and mandate.

On the other hand, history has shown time and again that neither a religion's dependence upon the state for legitimacy nor a religion combined with the forces of the state has served religion, the people or their society very well. As the Frenchman Alexis de Tocqueville wrote in 1835, "When it comes to state religions, I have always thought that, though they may perhaps sometimes momentarily serve the interests of political power, they are always sooner or later fatal for the church."

State religions and religious states are also fatal for the state and its citizens. We in Western society know as a result of, among other things, the Reformation, the French Revolution, and the

American experience that religion has never been successfully mediated through the state.

Religious believers must act *in* their governments, but not *through* them, for the business of the state requires deference to *expediency* and the maintenance of *power*. The power and purpose of religion involve truth and moral authority. These are the dividing lines between the true calling of religion in the state and its accommodation of and by political processes.

So long as there is a flicker of humanity in humankind, there will be belief, believers, and the great questions about our meaning in the universe. However, without the fundamental human right to express religious belief, the impact of such belief upon culture, with its moral conscience and mediation of power between the state and the individual, will be greatly diminished. And without this, it is much more difficult for people to answer the burning questions they have about God, the nature of their humanity, and their ultimate destiny, much less to weave their answers into the fabric of society.

THE POINT IS . . .

Back in 1859, when Charles Darwin went public with his theory of evolution, most Roman Catholics deemed Darwin a heretic. Then time passed. And by 1950, Pope Pius XII noted that evolution had become a "serious hypothesis . . . worthy of a more deeply studied investigation and reflection." Then more time passed. And just weeks ago, Pope John Paul II concluded that evolution is "more than just a theory."

My question is: What changed over the years? God either created the world as described in the Bible or He didn't. Whether the year is 1859 or 1998, a person could pick up a Bible and read the same account of Creation. The Bible hasn't changed. So why should our view of Creation change? Sadly, many religious leaders around the world have chosen to allow politically correct scientists to reign supreme over the timeless standard of God's Word.

The point is that we are slowly recreating a world without God—a world where God can conveniently be removed without anybody noticing. Already secular historians have removed any mention of God from our public school history books. And now, a major religious leader has given his blessing to remove God from the science books as well. Is it any wonder then that this next generation of children is growing up without a knowledge of God, without a belief in absolutes, and Âwithout a sense of hope?

Society in
Jeopardy

THE DIMINISHING CHURCH

Here's the church. Here's the steeple. Open the doors, and where are the people?

While it is true that millions of Americans attend church services each week, this number is decreasing annually. A mere 26 percent of adults under age thirty attend church weekly—down 8 percent in the past twenty years, according to a Roper poll. Even among adults aged thirty to sixty, the percentage attending church has declined 7 percent. But the church in America isn't just diminishing in size. What is even more disturbing is the church's diminishing influence in our society.

Historically, American churches have had a rich influence on our culture. This is no longer true. For many Americans, Christianity has simply become a cultural religion. This may be attributed to some church leaders who do little to nurture true spirituality in their members. Walk into many churches today, and you'll find self-righteous holy clubs. Instead of ministering to the world, these modern-day monasteries have withdrawn from it. And as they turn inward, far too many churches spend their time philosophizing among themselves instead of sending a message of salt and light.

John Stott, a British evangelical, observed that outsiders can easily sense whether a church is a refuge *from* them rather than *for* them. Ask many nonchurchgoers and they'll tell you the church can be a cold, unwelcoming place, its pews filled with Sunday-morning hypocrites. Sadly, this is far too often the truth. Many contemporary evangelicals practice neo-Phariseeism, which is evidenced in their retreat or separation from the rest of the world. And donning a facade of holiness, these separatists find it easy to thank God they are not like "other" people.

At the other extreme, there are Christians who are fixated with dominating the world by acquiring political power. Among those church leaders, many have sold out to the demands of tel-evangelism and have simply given their audience what it wants to hear by "tickling their ears." As a result, we see pastors "dumbing down" their sermons in an effort to appeal to the hearts and feelings of their flocks—instead of their heads and intellect.

British theologian H. G. Wood made a painfully accurate observation of the church when he noted, "Somehow the whole bottom has fallen out of our civilization. . . . It is the death, or deathlike swoon, of Christianity."

When the swooning began, it left a vacuum quickly filled by secularism. Secular thought so successfully transcended the cul-ture that practically every vestige of Christianity has now disap-peared from public life. Christianity has retreated to the private sphere where few can see or hear it and where its influence can be avoided. Meanwhile, America's secular society is systemati-cally closing the door to virtually all forms of Judeo-Christian expression in public places. This deliberate removal of religious symbols and expressions had, and will continue to have, a dev-astating effect on the American psyche. In a very real sense, we are witnessing the de-Christianization of America's soul, and it is happening at an alarming speed—like that of a firestorm wreak-ing destruction on a once reverent nation.

The only authentic response to the diminishing influence of Christianity is a return to true Christianity. The local church must lead the way. The Bible is clear that God does not call His church to retreat from the world, which means Christians shouldn't hide from the world's problems. Rather, the Gospel should propel Christians to be agents of spiritual and social change. God has placed the church on this earth for a reason. He calls it to engage the world, embrace its needs, and ultimately transform it for His glory.

THE POINT IS . . .

When you pull into your driveway after church on Sunday, have you ever noticed what your neighbors are doing? If it's a sunny day, chances are that they're outside mowing the lawn, playing with their kids, and getting some exercise. Odds are that they aren't coming home from church.

According to the Barna Research Group, church attendance has fallen to its lowest level in a decade. Specializing in church statistics, the Barna Group's survey revealed that 82 percent of adults call themselves religious, but only 37 percent of those surveyed attended worship services within the week before being polled. While 50 percent of Americans over fifty years old attend church regularly, only 31 percent of baby boomers attended church within the last week. And baby busters aren't breaking church attendance records, either. The problem is that the church is not meeting the needs of our younger generations and has become culturally irrelevant.

The point is that Jesus Christ IS culturally relevant—He meets the needs of all generations. During His time on earth, His conduct and conversations were innovative, fresh, and even trend-setting. But somewhere over the years, the church has forgotten the Master's ways. It has poured millions of dollars into building cathedrals instead of putting food into the mouths of the homeless, the widows, and the orphans. It has alienated our youth with legalistic rules and outdated outreaches. It's time to return to the Master's ways.

IS FRANCE OUR FUTURE?

There is no city on earth as full of the riches of Western culture as Paris. Despite this cultural wealth, however, Paris remains a place where anything goes, especially in the sexual realm. Majestic cathedrals designed to house thousands of worshipers stand empty, while pharmaceutical factories manufacturing the abortion pill RU-486 burn the midnight oil. Tourists strolling through the streets of Paris are more likely to see posters of nude women prominently displayed rather than flyers advertising a church service or religious publication.

Paris has become a place where churches and synagogues fail to speak to their people. In the rare instances where they do speak, people no longer care to listen because religion plays a minimal role—not only in Paris but also in the entire French society. While it's true that Catholicism, the primary religion of France, still exerts some influence on the nation's culture, it has little effect on its spirituality. Only 4 percent of the French population attend church services regularly. And less than 2 percent consider themselves evangelical Christians. Many of the French people boldly declare themselves atheists, and most institutions, whether government or private, are considered secular.

Yet religion wasn't always irrelevant to the French. Judeo-Christian values at one time permeated French culture. France was once dominated by the same Judeo-Christian principles on which our own nation was founded. Yet today, the French people have pushed God and religion out of the public sphere. The government is presently in the process of classifying different religions and reputable churches as cults. On a recent trip to France, I met a group of people who had a small Christian school that had been classified as a cult.

Such religious discrimination is no stranger to Paris. Female Muslim students have been forbidden to wear their head scarves to class. In 1993, members of the Christian Bible Church were arrested for their faith. Yet in the midst of this religious persecution, the French have done little to fight back—no doubt a sign that they believe religious freedom may not be worth the fight. In France, religion has retreated so far out of the public square that it may have trouble finding the road home.

Regrettably, America has strayed off course and wandered down the same dangerous path. Judging by the rate at which our courts and legislators have attempted to privatize religion, America may soon rid itself of religion's influence in our culture, too.

Gradually, the courts and legislation have been building a wall between church and state, rendering many religious people powerless to influence the morality of this country. Our public schools are not the only place where religious expression has come under attack. Courtrooms, the workplace, and even churches have been sanitized of religious expression as well.

Those who value religious and human freedom must reverse the retreat of religion from the public sphere or our churches may soon be no more than tourist attractions—and our country a nation that does not know God.

THE POINT IS . . .

What do you know about George Whitefield? If you're like the woman I recently spoke with at a Christian bookstore, you're saying, "George Whitefield? The name's not familiar to me. Sorry."

Today's church could learn a great deal from a young man named George Whitefield, who took the colonies by storm.

The year was 1738. Whitefield left his home in England to bring the Gospel to the "red Indians" in the colonies. Yet Whitefield quickly realized there were plenty of white colonists who needed the Gospel as well. So Whitefield started traveling and preaching. Wherever he preached, thousands upon thousands gathered to hear his dramatic and forthright presentation of the Gospel. Whitefield sought out those most in need, both spiritually and physically—the unchurched, the undesirables, and the needy. He preached in the mines. Miners were converted and mining conditions eventually improved. He preached in the countryside to the uneducated. Many more were converted and, before long, schools were built. Whenever Whitefield preached, souls were transformed. Wherever he preached, social change occurred.

The point is that the American church could learn a great deal from the life of George Whitefield. Sadly, as evidenced by a Christian bookstore clerk, we have forgotten his name as well as his lesson. His lesson: Jesus Christ transforms societies, not just souls. For the Gospel doesn't just change people's eternal destinies, it also dramatically affects how they live.

SUICIDE—
THE DESPAIR OF A CULTURE

Recently, a thirteen-year-old girl in England overdosed on sleeping pills and killed herself, leaving behind stunned and grieving parents. The horrified world immediately looked for a cause—and found one in a group of neighborhood bullies who had made the girl's life miserable.

The girl's youth and the fact that she was bullied into a tragic decision make this an especially horrifying case. Yet tragedies such as this are not uncommon. In the United States in 1995, 31,284 Americans ended their own lives—an average of eighty-five individuals each day. Shockingly, according to one report, there are more suicides than homicides in the United States.

Why do so many individuals choose to end their lives? In some cases, the cause seems evident—an abusive home life, low self-esteem, loss of a loved one, a major life change, ongoing depression, desertion, or divorce. The reasons are endless, but few seem sufficient for such an unalterable act.

I believe the problem lies deeper than these surface issues. I believe that the problem lies within the structure of our society itself, in the way we value human life.

Perhaps a once-popular bumper sticker sums up the current view of life: "The person who dies with the most toys, wins." Sadly, many people latch onto this whim and base their lives on it. Some work desperately for wealth, prestige, or power. Others substitute popularity, drug-induced highs, a new house, or even a family member as their focus for life.

Unfortunately, when the house burns down, the loved one leaves, the job is lost, the actor gets old, or the fan-seekers look for a new idol, people discover that they have ended up with nothing.

It's easy to blame suicide victims. But haven't we, as a society, helped drive them to it? We've suggested that their value is measured in their achievements. When they fail, we reject them. When they succeed, we envy them. We build friendships for the purpose of "networking" or "career advancement," whether for a job or a place on the homecoming court. Yet where are we when our "friend" becomes an outcast? We have devalued the dignity of those we deem not useful to us, whether they are the unborn, elderly, handicapped, or ill; in the process, we have devalued ourselves.

Last, but most importantly, we have taken away God. Ultimately, religion is the source of human dignity, of individual value. Christianity gave people something worth living for—they once knew that life was a gift to be lived for a purpose and that it would have an eternal effect. They knew that, no matter how tough things were, good could come from it. They knew that, no matter what others thought of them, they had value. This faith gave them purpose and courage to face the challenges of life.

Our replacements for God have been a dismal failure. Only by turning away from the false solutions and looking for true answers in the place we originally found them can we have long-term hope for our society. Suicide is not the problem of a few dysfunctional individuals. It is our problem as a country, as a community, as neighbors, and as friends.

THE POINT IS . . .

When NASA announced the discovery of life on Mars, what thoughts ran through your head? Did you conjure up images of flying saucers?

Or of alien space creatures? Or of God laughing at how self-centered we are to think that Earth is the only world He created?

Whatever your thoughts, chances are you didn't voice them aloud to anyone, or at least not to anyone outside your family. But while it used to be that those who believed in the extraterrestrial were considered nut cases, Time reports that 40 percent of Americans now believe UFOs are "real."

Why are so many ordinarily skeptical Americans willing to believe in life outside of Earth? Because so many Americans are seeking meaning, purpose, and a sense of connectedness. In an age when media experts and advertising gurus make us feel like pieces of plastic, people are quick to embrace anything spiritual—whether it be the occult, angels, UFOs, or extraterrestrial beings. That's why the idea of life on other planets seems plausible, likely, and perhaps even comforting to so many seeking a place in this world or universe.

The point is that people are looking outside of Christianity for meaning and transcendence. What has changed? Jesus Christ hasn't. But His church has. Choosing to stay tucked away from the world, modern Christianity has all but faded into a black hole.

A POPULAR
HOLIDAY

What's the most popular holiday in the United States? Ask my children and they will answer, "Christmas, of course!" But what may surprise you is that the runner-up for the most popular holiday is Halloween. Recently, when members of the media compared U.S. retailers' reports for different holiday merchandise, they concluded that, while Christmas goods brought in the biggest bucks, Halloween items remain big business, too.

It comes as no surprise that Christmas is so popular. After all, it's a holiday about good news, hope, and ultimately about Christ, the Prince of Peace. Even people who aren't Christians celebrate Christmas—and not just because of Santa Claus. Christmas is a holiday that softens the hardest of hearts and transforms lives for the better.

Yet Halloween's red-letter date is in stark contrast to such potential for positive change. While regarded in a secular culture as a holiday, sadly, it is more a celebration of fear and, ultimately, a grim reminder about death. Halloween is a day when it's okay for adults to scare children, luring them into houses with promises of treats, while tricking them with frightening music. Mainstream America purchases hideous masks and decorates its doorsteps with images of vampires and ghosts. And vandalism and other unprosecuted crimes abound in communities across the land. Even the workplace throws off the restraints of professional decorum and allows employees to "dress up" for the occasion.

It's easy to identify one of the reasons for Halloween's #2 ranking. This is the mass marketing of the custom by America's public schools. Administrators and teachers often don costumes, and chaotic parties often follow, where the educational value of the activity comes into serious question. While room mothers bake cupcakes shaped like ghosts, goblins, and demons and cardboard characters breathe fiery venom, the once-trusted teacher becomes the wicked witch—all set before a captive, if not confused, audience of unknowing children. In most so-called celebrations, there is usually no note sent home in advance for students who may desire to opt-out of this "celebration." Year in and year out, unknowing parents and their children are being processed to participate in and claim this nationally accepted holiday.

Fast-forward six weeks to December where the "Winter Holidays" are now celebrated in this same public building. Tour the hallways and you will find few, if any, traditional or religious symbols of Christmas. Afraid to express themselves, or ignorant of the legality of religion in the schools, many of these same teachers are not as anxious to celebrate now as they were on Halloween. Gone is the nostalgic ritual of sustaining the cultural traditions of centuries past. If a student or employee is courageous enough to decorate a tree, neutral instructors will recommend a reindeer or a multicultural symbol of another major world religion. The chaos that now transcends the classroom is one of great care to balance out the equal treatment of "holidays." Gone, too, are the favorite Yuletide carols at the school program or company party, and the once-festive occasion now rings hollow with the eerie emptiness of real substance.

The American public as a whole has been falsely led to believe they cannot even mention the word *Christmas* in the public forum. But when it comes to Halloween, the irony is found in the orange and black cutouts of symbolized evil that ceremoniously go up on October 1. "Happy Halloween" choruses echo the paganistic pomp and circumstance now permeating our pop culture. From shopping centers to school auditoriums, Halloween could soon earn the #1 berth for most popular *and* most expensive American holiday.

Yet the public school and workplace promotion of Halloween is just the tip of the iceberg. The real indicator of cultural depravity is the realization that people are looking for an escape. Unfortunately, Halloween can only provide a temporary diversion in a world where there is little good news. Factor in the threat of lawsuits and ambiguity from the courts about the legal limits of celebrating Christmas, and it's understandable why America has cashed in Christ's birth for a one-night stand called Halloween. Halloween's growing popularity reminds us of the temptation that lurks in the darker side of our minds and lives.

The challenge to our personal freedom is to resist the culture's agenda to celebrate humanity's darkness. Some have argued that this popular holiday has true theological tenets in its markedly religious agents of pagan rituals. I wonder how many schoolteachers have examined this facet of the holiday.

THE POINT IS . . .

_____

Persecution of religious students in the schools takes many different forms. Many of the cases we see involve students who want to do something but aren't permitted. But when it comes to Halloween in school, the cases revolve around students who don't *want to do something— namely, participate in objectionable activities. This is a violation of their rights under the Constitution and Supreme Court ruling, and The Rutherford Institute handles many of their cases.*

For example, in California two second graders were harassed by their teacher because of their views on Halloween. They told the teacher they didn't want to participate in Halloween activities because

of their Christian views. Not only did the teacher make them participate, she also made fun of them in front of the class. Then, in West
Virginia, a third grader with Tourette's syndrome was read scary stories by his teacher on Halloween. Even though the stories bothered the
boy and aggravated his condition, the teacher read them anyway.

In another instance, a Spanish class in Michigan planned to celebrate the Spanish version of Halloween, the "Day of the Dead." The
students were supposed to bring in names of their dead relatives, so they
could summon their spirits during class. A mother with religious objections opted her child out of this exercise.

The point is, forcing children to participate in Halloween activities
without parental notification or consent violates your rights as a parent. You need to know about Halloween in the schools and your rights
as well as your children's rights.

WHICH UNBORN BABIES COUNT?

There's something I've been trying to figure out for a while—namely, which unborn babies count?

Although this seems like a straightforward question, it causes a lot of confusion and evokes much emotion. Social situations can be confusing. When a woman announces she's pregnant, it is no longer clear how to respond. For if a couple tries repeatedly to get pregnant, they are congratulated on their success. Yet when an unmarried teen admits to her classmates that she is pregnant, well-meaning friends offer her a ride to the local abortion clinic.

Legal situations aren't much clearer. A just conceived fetus has the legal right to inherit property and money. And in a move to protect the health of unborn babies, states are beginning to charge expectant mothers who abuse drugs and alcohol with child abuse. Yet that same fetus may be legally killed if the mother-to-be resents putting on "unwanted weight" or doesn't want to bear the financial burden of raising another child.

How do we, as a society, decide which unborn babies count? The answer might be found in Corpus Christi, Texas, where one evening a drunk driver crashed his truck into a car driven by Jeannie Coronado as she returned from a trip to the local market. Her car was carrying bags full of groceries, and in her womb she carried a baby.

Jeannie was rushed to the hospital and gave birth by emergency C-section to a baby girl, Krystal. But Krystal was born prematurely, at just seven and a half months, and with a birth weight of only four pounds. She also suffered extensive brain damage. Two days later, baby Krystal died.

The case went to court, where a jury convicted the driver—whose blood-alcohol level was more than twice the legal limit—of intoxication manslaughter. He was sentenced to sixteen years in jail because a jury of his peers held this drunk driver criminally liable for fatally harming an unborn baby.

Why did this unborn baby's life count? Why did it count to this community in Texas? Why did it count to the jury seated in that particular courtroom? This life counted because baby Krystal was wanted. And because baby Krystal's parents wanted her, they suffered a great loss upon her death. The truth is that whenever an unborn baby dies, there is loss, whether or not the parents feel it or society admits it. Tragically, in our legal system and our society, only lives that are valued by others seem to count.

In America, there is only one difference between a person aborting an unborn baby and a person driving a car into an unborn one. One baby was wanted, the other was not. Both babies died. Both babies lost out on life. Yet somehow, in this world in which we live, a wanted baby's life has more value than an unwanted one—or so we try to convince ourselves.

But even the most persuasive arguments fall short if they fail to recognize the great value of the lives of all unborn babies—wanted or not. For it is the Creator of life who determines value and worth, and He has deemed all human life sacred. Who are we to argue?

THE POINT IS . . .

Children grow up way too fast these days. If you're a parent, I'm sure you sometimes shield your child from certain harsh realities. After all, it's best if children don't know certain facts too soon. Many things will scare a child who's too young to understand them.

For example, in California, two young children saw something they never should have seen. The children were playing in a field when they came across a makeshift casket sealed with duct tape. Not knowing what it was, they looked inside. And there lay five cardboard boxes containing forty-five discarded fetuses—recognizable as human babies—some at over twenty weeks' gestation.

The San Bernardino Sheriff's Department began an investigation for possible criminal activity. The coroner's office concluded that the babies were all "legally aborted." But California has strict laws to regulate the transportation of what the abortion industry calls the "products of conception." The forty-five fetuses were traced to an abortion clinic in Los Angeles. Authorities are still searching for the person responsible for the illegal transportation.

The point is that the only reason the abortion industry thrives is because there's a widespread contempt for life in our society. What kind of world do we live in where babies are aborted and discarded like useless trash? How would you explain this to your child?

THE RIGHT TO LIFE

When Susan Smith rolled her car into a pond in South Carolina, she committed the worst kind of child abuse—murder. The horrific image of two little boys strapped down in car seats, slowly sinking to their deaths, cruelly etched itself into our minds. The infamous pond of death became a memorial where Americans flocked to pay tribute to the innocent children who died such an unjust death—at the hands of the one they called "Mommy."

Many found it hard to feel anything but anger toward Susan Smith. For not only did she murder two children, she murdered her *own* children. Regardless of her reasons or mental state, Susan Smith was without excuse because there is no excuse for the taking of innocent life. Yet the killing of children at the hands of their own mothers continues.

When Melissa Drexler allegedly strangled her newborn baby boy in a bathroom stall during her senior prom, she also committed the worst kind of child abuse—murder. The painful image of a newborn baby staring at his mother for the first time as she struggled to end his life is not easily forgotten.

To many people, the Melissa Drexler story is more of a tragedy than a crime. What kind of a nation do we live in where teenage mothers care more about returning to the dance floor than nurturing their newborn? We are horrified that a high-school senior dumped her strangled newborn in the trash can, but Melissa's youth seems to have earned her some sympathy.

Regardless of her age, however, Melissa Drexler was without excuse. For there is no excuse for the taking of innocent life. Yet the killing continues.

When a woman takes RU-486 to make her uterus contract strongly enough to expel her unborn baby, she, too, is committing the worst kind of child abuse. The helpless image of a miniature baby boy or girl covered with blood will be forever imprinted in the woman's mind, heart, and soul. Yet no American will ever pay tribute to this unborn baby.

Perhaps it is because no one, except the woman and her doctor, knew that the baby ever existed. No one, except the woman and her doctor, ever knew his tiny heart was beating or that he had a habit of sucking his thumb. Our Supreme Court had decided that his life wasn't anyone's business except his mother's. It was her body—her choice.

For many, this woman's story is neither a crime nor a tragedy. It's simply a choice.

Many believe that while abortion may not be a great idea, there are times when it may be the best choice for a pregnancy. They convince themselves that the abortion was in the best interests of the baby.

Regardless of whether we call it a crime, a tragedy, or a choice, the trashing of children's lives—by the hands of their mothers or anyone else—will continue until we publicly acknowledge and act on what we already know is true. Children, babies, even unborn babies, are worthy of not just protection but the right that God gives us all—the right to life.

THE POINT IS . . .

Ever since the Supreme Court's 1973 ruling in Roe v. Wade, *the debate about abortion has raged. But few commentators ask the question at*

the core of the issue: Is there really a "right" to abortion? A Michigan
Court of Appeals answered, "No."

At issue was whether the state could require a twenty-four hour
waiting period before a woman gives her informed consent to abortion.
The Michigan judges found no support for the conclusion that there is
an inalienable "right" to have an abortion—even after examining the
state drafters' intent and reviewing Supreme Court precedent. The court
noted that abortion was in fact a criminal offense in 1963, the year the
state constitution was adopted. The judges reasoned that since the state
constitution is silent on this issue, the drafters had no intention of alter-
ing existing law by inventing a new "right" to abortion.

But while cases like this one are being won at the state level,
President Clinton still refuses to accept a ban on partial-birth abortions.
Apparently, in our nation's capital, the message that abortion is not a
basic human right hasn't hit home.

The point is that the framers of our federal and state constitutions
never imagined that people would one day invent a new "right" called
abortion. But while certain freedoms, such as life for the unborn, were
fractured with Roe v. Wade, we can still exercise our free speech
rights—and voice our pro-life views.

THE ROAD
TO AN AMERICAN HOLOCAUST

Katherine strained to read the chalkboard. Ingrid hadn't learned her catechism well enough. Martha had parents from two different racial backgrounds. Mary was mentally ill, while Lovisa was considered "antisocial." What do these women have in common? They were all forcibly sterilized in Sweden's effort to create a genetically pure super race.

Sweden was a dangerous place to live from 1934 to 1974 for young women such as these. During that forty-year period, the Swedish authorities forcibly sterilized 62,000 of their citizens, primarily women, as part of their plan to create a master race. The sterilizations, routinely accepted in Sweden, were first performed on mentally ill patients. Later, the government extended the process to include other individuals deemed "unfit" to be parents.

Now the Swedish government is horrified and embarrassed and plans to conduct an inquiry into this dark page of history. Meanwhile, Americans who hear the story breathe a sigh of relief that we do not live in a country where such horrific scientific experiments occur. Yet before we rest too easily, consider these situations:

Jenny sits in her doctor's office, stunned with the news that her unborn child has a serious genetic disease. Her doctor suggests that she terminate the pregnancy. Meanwhile, Grandma

Marie is unconscious at the nursing home; her family decides to stop administering food and water so she will starve to death. Both these situations occur, with rising frequency, in our own homeland.

Meanwhile, in various political forums across the county, certain doctors and scientists are trying to persuade their constituents to allow experimental research on human embryos, the mentally ill, the elderly, patients with Parkinson's disease, and others who cannot give their consent—even though the research would not benefit the victim at all. One such proposed statute in Maryland would allow high-risk, nontherapeutic research on "decisionally incapacitated" patients, for the advancement of science. The experiments may be painful or fatal. The patient is offered no compensation for harm or injury. No researchers or physicians would be held liable for any injury. The victim could be enrolled, without his or her knowledge, by health-care agents or anyone else appointed as a surrogate.

We have already stripped away the dignity of the unborn and many elderly. This new movement simply relegates yet another vulnerable group of people to a subhuman status.

How have we gotten to this point? It's been reached one step at a time through a gradual, logical progression. Once Americans assumed they had the right to deny future generations their right to live, it logically followed that we have the right to choose who is to die. By applying dehumanizing terminology such as *the product of a pregnancy,* we have distanced ourselves from other people, helpless people. Human beings have become disposable. We are now beyond the thinkable in the areas of abortion, infanticide, euthanasia, and scientific experimentation. No one is safe.

As Americans, as religious persons, as human beings, we can no longer afford to remain silent. Anyone can vote, write his or her congressperson, petition. Those who are able can run for political office. Others can reach out with love to young, frightened mothers or those caring for a member of the family who is ill. Neighbors can offer to help those whose burdens seem too great to bear. Countless avenues of opportunity abound. The slippery slide into an American holocaust can still be stopped.

THE POINT IS . . .

Between March and July of 1998, your tax dollars provided fifty million condoms, five hundred thousand intrauterine devices, and 4.8 million cycles of contraceptive pills to men and women in sixty countries.

At President Clinton's urging, the Senate recently voted fifty-three to forty-six to approve the early release of $385 million in foreign family planning funds. Some of this money will undoubtedly go to organizations that use abortion as a means of family planning, including the International Planned Parenthood Federation. Under the Reagan and Bush administrations, no organization that performed or subsidized abortion could receive United States tax funds. However, when Bill Clinton became president, he reversed this policy. In Clinton's passionate appeal for the early release of these funds, he argued that family planning programs were being hurt by the delay in funding.

The point is that American tax dollars could well increase the number of abortions around the world. Technically, current law bars organizations that receive American family planning funds from spending those dollars on abortions. Yet pro-life activists suspect the tax dollars given to pro-abortion groups will—directly or indirectly—fund abortions internationally. Is this how you want your hard-earned money spent—to fund abortions for women in foreign countries? If not, then express your concern to your senator—it's your right and duty as a citizen.

WOMEN DESERVE MORE

Women deserve more than the pro-choice movement has to offer. When the movement celebrated the twenty-fourth anniversary of *Roe v. Wade* in 1997, Hillary Rodham Clinton echoed the president's desire that abortion should remain "safe, legal, and rare."

Both Bill and Hillary Clinton apparently believe they have women's best interests at heart when they support pro-choice policies. It's not that they *support* abortion, the Clintons insist. Rather, their concern is to safeguard the rights and health of women.

But women don't need this kind of protection. What they need is the truth. In this day of legalized abortion-on-demand, abortion is far from safe and rare. If the truth be told, abortion and death go hand in hand. Abortion is not only a fatal health hazard for the unwanted fetus, it poses serious, possibly fatal, medical risks to the woman as well.

At least 100 physical complications have been associated with abortion, including immediate problems like hemorrhage, infection, and blood clots, and long-term effects, including future sterility, stillbirth, and miscarriage. Resulting psychological problems range from disturbing memories and sleep disorders to depression and guilt.

Unlike many medical procedures, women considering an

abortion are rarely informed of the risks. Most women turn to abortion to solve the problem of an unwanted pregnancy, but they don't learn about the potential dangers to their own bodies until it is too late.

Take the case of twenty-six-year-old "Betty," who entered an abortion clinic for a third-trimester abortion. During the procedure, the doctor failed to remove the entire fetus. Instead, he packed Betty's vagina with gauze, gave her shots and pills, and instructed her to place any discharged fetal remnants in a bag and bring them to him later. Betty never had that opportunity. She died from an infection resulting from her "safe" abortion.

Then there was fourteen-year-old "Gwen," a mere child carrying a child. Gwen opted to have an abortion, and the procedure went off without a hitch—except that four days later Gwen began experiencing stomach pains, vomiting, and running a high fever. On day five, Gwen's mother found her fourteen-year-old daughter dead on the bathroom floor—a casualty of her "routine" abortion.

"Sharon" had every expectation that her abortion would be simple. Yet complications arose when the doctor noticed a clogged suction tube and then a punctured uterus and severed small intestine. Sharon lost all but about five-and-a-half inches of her small intestine, both Fallopian tubes, her appendix, and a portion of her large intestine.

Sharon now lives with a permanent catheter tube implanted to allow nutrients to enter her bloodstream fourteen hours every day—for the rest of her life. According to her abortion provider, the life-threatening injuries Sharon sustained are just "one of the complications of this procedure that happen from time to time."

Sadly, the public rarely reads about complications from abortion because such cases go largely unreported and unpublished. These tragic stories cry out for review by anyone who adamantly supports a woman's "right" to choose, including President

Clinton and his wife. Women deserve more. They deserve the truth.

THE POINT IS . . .

When it comes to respect and status, women have indeed come a long way. It's true that the family and the local church have a patriarchal structure, but when it comes to salvation, there is neither male nor female. Why? Because every human being, male and female, is created in the image of God. And all stand in need of forgiveness.

But let me make myself perfectly clear; this isn't to say there are no differences between men and women. Just the opposite. True equality leads to a respect for differences between men and women. Unfortunately, some are calling for the elimination of gender distinctions arguing that gender and sex are a state of mind, not physical characteristics. Anyone can assume the role of a man or woman, or both.

These ideas are not the answer to the oppression of women. Though many of today's movements promise freedom, choice, and empowerment to all women, they lead to the further erosion of the traditional family and the sanctity of human life. The real answer to this oppression is Jesus Christ, for there is no Christian justification for the domination of one group by another. And during His time on earth, Christ sought to free women from many of the existing social and religious restrictions.

COMMERCIALIZING CHRISTMAS— HAVE WE MISSED THE POINT?

Even before the Thanksgiving turkey was finished, moms and dads were pounding the pavement in search of the "must-have" Christmas toys of the upcoming shopping season. They nabbed fantasy action figures, Holiday Barbies, plush toys that snore, and interactive Barneys that play peekaboo. Some even purchased cyberpets, special computer-chip pets whose young owners must feed and clean up after them to keep them alive.

As a further aid to shopping parents, multiple Santa Clauses suddenly appeared in the malls, ready to hear the confidences of small children who knew exactly what they wanted to find under the tree on Christmas morning. The children's wish lists were pretty straightforward. They wanted what their friends already had or what all the other children on TV enjoyed so much.

In light of the response to the hot toys of the season, toy manufacturers happily estimated that the value of toys shipped in 1997 would even exceed the previous year's total. And although they expected some items to be out of stock before Thanksgiving, they planned to have enough other popular toys on hand to satisfy anxious parents.

Meanwhile, even the schools where children spend so much of their learning time seem to miss the whole point of the holiday. Some school boards plan programs that omit all traditional Christian carols. Others forbid "Merry Christmas" signs and replace the greeting with "Happy Holidays." One school even outlawed the color green, saying it was a "Christian color."

One case that highlights this extreme Christmas phobia involves a high-school student who received an assignment to present a five-minute video on the true meaning of Christmas. Because the video mentioned Christ, however, his project was rejected. I have yet to understand how anyone could discuss the true meaning of Christmas without referring to Christ. Surely, something is wrong when America's children are encouraged to celebrate the fictional Rudolph but refused the opportunity to discuss the historical Jesus.

To claim that Christmas is something other than it is—a holiday with religious (Christian) foundations—is dishonest.

Somehow, I find this entire process discouraging and disheartening. In a society already known for its selfishness and consumerism, it seems that a religious holiday would be a good opportunity to celebrate something else—something wholesome and good. Rather than making it the height of the selling season, why can't it be a season for celebrating family and friendship, camaraderie and memories? Why can't it be a season of reflection and holy joy? Why can't it be a time to step back and meditate on the original reasons behind the holiday?

Fortunately, we still live in a country where families can celebrate their religious holidays with freedom. We can still attend religious services, set up manger scenes, and sing Christmas carols. We can still read the Christmas story to our children and talk about the travels of the Wise Men (who, according to the Christmas cards, "still seek Him"). We can divert the focus, in our own homes at least, from a "gimme" attitude to a sharing spirit. And we can recapture an awe and gratitude for the greatest Gift ever given to man—the coming of God's Holy Son as a light into a dark world.

THE POINT IS . . .

For you, Christmas may have already become a distant memory. But for Patricia Coons, it will always hold a special place in her heart. That's because in 1996, Patricia Coons learned a valuable lesson about taking a stand for her religious freedom. Patricia works in the payroll division for Contra Costa County, California. Each year at Christmastime, Patricia brings in a nativity scene from home and places it on her desk. But back in 1995, Patricia's supervisor told her to remove the nativity scene and threatened her with disciplinary action. So this past Christmas, Patricia took preemptive action to ensure the baby Jesus would have room on her desk. Earlier in the year, Patricia contacted The Rutherford Institute. Our attorneys sent a letter to county officials, outlining the rights of religious persons to display holiday decorations at work. As a result, the department changed its holiday policy and now allows Patricia and other employees to display nativity scenes and even play Christmas music.

The point is that the government must accommodate the religious beliefs of its employees. We hope that Contra Costa County and other government agencies will extend the spirit of Christmas into the new year by recognizing the rights of religious persons three hundred and sixty-five days a year.

THANKSGIVING— AMERICAN STYLE

On a sunny fall day in 1621, Governor William Bradford declared a day of public thanksgiving for the tiny colony of settlers at Cape Cod.

After a long, desperate winter, almost half of the Pilgrims' original party had died. The rest struggled all summer to provide for their basic needs. Aided by the help of a friendly Indian who spoke English and knew how to live in the hostile new land, the Pilgrims' efforts had been rewarded. Now the small party looked toward their second winter, hoping their limited rations would bring them through. With grateful hearts, they invited ninety Indian neighbors to celebrate with them and give thanks to God with a feast that lasted three full days. Finally, they had found a land free from religious persecution, and God was helping them to make it home.

Over 375 years later, school children find themselves in halls lined with pictures of sober, black-coated Pilgrims, and fat, colorful turkeys. Art class becomes an exciting event as youngsters make paper Indian headdresses with yellow and orange feathers. On the actual day itself, families gather together to feast on home-cooked meals and relax. The next day, thousands of consumers crowd the streets in a buying frenzy.

Somehow, this celebration of the holiday makes me uneasy. As I look across the newspapers and legal cases that find their way to our office, my concern grows stronger.

I discovered that a teacher's contract has not been renewed because she allowed her class to perform a play and discuss the religious persecution of the Pilgrims. The principal who attended the play acted particularly agitated when the students talked about what they were thankful for.

Another school district denied a church the right to rent a school building for its annual Thanksgiving dinner. The district had determined it would no longer lease to religious organizations.

A university professor decided that Thanksgiving is not a religious holiday. Because the professor disagreed with a student's perspective, the student received a poor grade on a history paper.

A post office employee was rebuked for posting a speech by George Washington that mentions God. Although there were posters displayed for Native American Awareness month and Santa Claus for Christmas, there were complaints about the Thanksgiving posters.

A church that feeds the homeless was ordered to seek new zoning and get permits to operate as a social service agency rather than a church. The pastor believes the city is attempting to close down the program. Last year, the same city tried to ban outdoor meal programs for the homeless.

Perhaps the saddest case is that of a teacher who posted a bulletin board titled "Thank you, God, for . . ." She then added pictures of things children are thankful for. While the teacher was busy in class, her assistant principal took scissors and cut out the word "God."

Thanksgiving—American style. Somehow, I have the nagging feeling that something is missing.

THE POINT IS . . .

Desiree Alexander is a six-year-old girl who loves God. Desiree's desire is to share God's love with her classmates at Eastern Elementary

School in Hagerstown, Maryland, and that's exactly what she did one day during recess. Apparently Desiree's classmates didn't respond very well, and her teacher responded even worse. Desiree told her parents that her first grade teacher pulled her aside and warned her NEVER to talk about Jesus in the public school. Desiree was crushed. At her parents' request, The Rutherford Institute asked that the first grade teacher apologize to Desiree. In addition, we requested that all the teachers receive an elementary lesson in religious freedom. I am pleased to report that the teachers proved to be quick learners. In a settlement, the school's attorney admitted that Desiree had the law on her side and took steps to ensure that the teachers would comply with the First Amendment.

The point of law is that student-initiated religious expression is allowed in public school during noninstructional time, such as recess.

When I hear stories like Desiree's, I am always struck by the determination, boldness, and courage that children have when it comes to standing up for their faith. As parents, we have the responsibility to do everything in our power to encourage and not squelch these traits. And we would be wise to emulate them as well.

WHAT *SEINFELD* SAYS ABOUT AMERICA

After one of the most successful runs in television history, Jerry Seinfeld decided to pull the plug on his self-titled sitcom that anchored NBC's ubiquitous "Must See TV." The news was reported on the front page of the *New York Times* and made the cover of *Time*. The final episode was viewed by over seventy million people.

Seinfeld's gimmick is famous—it's a show about the quirks we notice in people but never really stop to analyze. Episodes featured idiosyncratic characters like the "close-talker"—that person who always seems to violate your personal space. Essentially, the show is about nothing. Its characters aren't going anywhere or trying to do anything other than survive with minimal effort.

And they are famously self-absorbed. At the end of one recent season, the character George, played by Jason Alexander, is engaged to be married. He wants to break off the engagement but is too weak to be honest. In the season's final episode, his fiancée dies from licking toxic envelopes for the wedding invitations. But George isn't sad about her death—he's relieved that the engagement is off.

In episode after episode, the characters in *Seinfeld* reveal that they're willing to do just about anything to serve their own interests, no matter the moral or ethical issues involved.

Unfortunately, when one looks around today's America, some television isn't very far removed from real life.

But while the characters he created are narcissistic nihilists, Jerry Seinfeld isn't to blame for the moral decay in American life and culture. As *Washington Post* TV critic Tom Shales says, "*Seinfeld* is about the human condition. And the human condition is basically a mess." In other words, America lost its values first—*Seinfeld* is so popular because it mocks her condition in such expert fashion.

Consider the episode involving George's engagement. It isn't much of a stretch to see the parallel between George's concern for convenience in his own life—even at the expense of the life of another—and the abortion issue. Personal convenience at the expense of life is at the heart of the abortion debate. Of course, the writers of that episode probably never considered the connection. But because they are so attuned to the *zeitgeist* of the age, their show reflected the theme.

Jerry Seinfeld also focused in on America's ambivalence about homosexuality. He coined the now-famous catch phrase "not that there's anything wrong with that" in reference to gay characters on the show. This statement reflected American society's surface desire to be tolerant toward homosexuals, but by its very utterance revealed the uncertainty of a speaker who deep down wasn't quite sure his statement was true. In an ironic sense, it's as if Seinfeld meant the opposite of what he said.

Sometime early in the next millennium, *Seinfeld's* relevance to American society will have diminished. Its quirky episodes will have grown stale through countless reruns. But if historians, ethicists, or anthropologists ever want to take the temperature of American society in the 1990s, they'll have nine years' worth of sitcom thermometer to measure by.

THE POINT IS . . .

What's your favorite television show? If you are like many Americans,
ER, Seinfeld, *and* Friends *rank up there among your favorites. But have
you ever turned on one of these shows, started laughing at a scene, and
then, in an uncomfortable moment, remembered that your child was
with you in the room also watching the show? As you grab the remote
control, you vow to stop watching trashy TV. But it's increasingly difficult to avoid the barrage of sexual scenes and innuendoes on prime-
time television.*

A recent issue of U.S. News & World Report *stated that during
prime time, a sexual act or reference occurs, on average, every four minutes; portrayals of premarital sex outnumbered sex within marriage by
eight to one; and casual sex is almost always condoned.* ER's *star pedi-
atrician, Doug Ross, can't seem to spend a Thursday night without a
new partner. A recent* Seinfeld *episode centered around Elaine's short-
age of contraceptive sponges. And* Friends *gives prominent airtime to
a lesbian couple parenting a baby.*

*The point is that television's obsession with sex is both a cause and
an effect of our society's view of sex. And if you regularly watch prime-
time TV, it will affect your view, too.*

GOVERNMENTAL
POWER

FORFEITING FREEDOM
IN THE NAME OF SECURITY

They fight "in the air, on land, and sea." They train to protect and to kill. They are the United States Marines. But should their job include drug surveillance on the U.S.-Mexican border? That is the question many are asking after the shooting death of a young Texas goat herder in May 1997.

Ezequiel Hernandez, Jr., eighteen, was described by friends as hard-working and well-liked. He helped herd goats as part of a church project and carried a rifle to protect them. Sometimes he shot at targets. On May 20, however, the teenager was shot and killed when he ran afoul of a heavily-camouflaged Marine unit assigned to patrol the U.S.–Mexican border. The unit was part of a drug-surveillance team working in cooperation with the Immigration and Naturalization Service's Border Patrol.

The Marines claimed they fired in self-defense. Others believe the young man was target practicing and did not see the soldiers. A West Texas grand jury declined to indict the Marines for murder, since the soldiers appeared to be following the rules of engagement. Yet many still wonder what really happened on that sad afternoon south of El Paso.

For many Americans, this tragic mix-up is yet another example of governmental power overstepping its bounds. Whether or not Hernandez did fire at the soldiers, the question remains: should the Marines have been there at all?

The most obvious reason to refrain from using military personnel for missions on American soil is that the military forces are trained for combat. The Marines may well have been operating by their training for combat situations when they fired on Hernandez. However, the country around Redford, Texas, is not a combat zone. The use of combat forces for noncombat situations leaves a large margin for error. One official admitted that the tragedy might not have occurred if the border had been patrolled by civilian law enforcement agencies.

The increasing use of military personnel and/or camouflaged special agents or storm troopers also frightens innocent people. It is one thing to have an army defend a country. It is something else to use the military against fellow citizens. As a result of incidents such as the Texas shooting, many Americans feel threatened by their government—not protected. According to polls conducted shortly after the Oklahoma City bombing, between 39 and 52 percent of Americans believed the federal government had become so powerful it was a threat to freedom.

The United States is one of the few nations whose politicians are elected by the people to be public servants. Bound by the Constitution, American officials have limited power to be used for the good of the people they represent.

When this power is used in a way that strikes fear into law-abiding American citizens, it is misused.

Unfortunately, one need look no further than the twentieth century for examples of governments that used violence to rule. As a result, millions of people were tortured, maimed, and murdered during the regimes of Pol Pot and the Khmer Rouge, Saddam Hussein, Mao Tse-tung, Stalin, Hitler, and others. These attempts to rule by ruthless force brought even greater violence and terror than the governments they replaced.

No one doubts the need for national security or for prevention of drug trafficking. Before we turn to our military for internal protection, though, we need to decide where to draw the line.

Do we really want martial law to assure our security? Before we trade our freedom for security, we need to take a long, close look at the cost.

THE POINT IS . . .

You're on your way to a big job interview when you realize you forgot something—something very important. You slam on your brakes, turn your car around, and rush back home to get it. What could be so important that you can't get a job without it? Not your briefcase, your power suit, or even your resumé. Instead, it's a small identification card. And if government officials have their way, you just might need to carry one with you to your next job interview.

With the supposed goal of cracking down on illegal immigration, the United States Senate voted to accept legislation that would create a central database to identify citizens and legal residents. This legislation would allow employers to call a government office and verify legal residency of a potential employee, thus making it more difficult for illegal immigrants to find work. To many Americans, the idea conjures up unwelcomed images of Big Brother intruding further into their lives.

The point is that many Americans are willing to trade their freedom for the promise of safety and security. They want to keep jobs in the hands of Americans and crime outside the borders of the United States at virtually any cost. But if this means having a national ID card before you can get a job, some may find the cost too high.

TECHNIQUES OF TYRANNY: A TERRIBLE TRADE

If the government promised to keep you safe from terrorism, drugs, and crime, would you give it more power over your life? If you are like the majority of Americans, your answer is an unqualified "yes."

As these societal ills continue to escalate, the average American feels frustrated and powerless, no longer able to insulate himself from random acts of violence and the effects of cultural decline. The result is a willingness to hand over the reins of autonomy to the government in the desperate hope that it can restore a safer social climate.

According to a recent poll, 70 percent of Americans would give up their Fourth Amendment right against unreasonable search and seizure to stop terrorism. Yet terrorism marches on. In Oklahoma, a bomb devastated a federal building, killing innocent men, women, and children. In Saudi Arabia, a terrorist bombing took the lives of nineteen Americans. And during the 1996 Summer Olympics in Atlanta, a pipe bomb wounded over 100 people, two fatally. Each of these acts has driven home Americans' powerlessness in the face of terrorism.

Even the president of the United States is not immune. Fearing a possible threat to his safety, his security forces closed off Pennsylvania Avenue in front of the White House by erecting barricades. These physical barriers between a government and her people symbolized the lengths to which Americans were willing to go to protect themselves from terrorism.

President Clinton then called for expanded government powers to help fight domestic terrorism. In effect, his proposed legislation would increase police powers and the FBI's ability to monitor and infiltrate groups suspected of terrorism, including wiretap authority, roving wiretaps on multiple phones, and the addition of one thousand new law enforcement agents.

To some, it seemed like a good trade: handing over freedom for a feeling of national safety, even if the feeling was fleeting.

So the trading continues, as the United States government applies similar policies to teens. In an attempt to curb violence by teens and on teens, local communities imposed curfews on its youth population. Since 1990, one fourth of the nation's 200 largest cities have instituted curfews. And to address the problem of teen drug abuse, the government legalized random drug tests in public schools.

The United States Supreme Court backed this philosophy of control when it ruled that public schools may legally conduct drug tests on student athletes. This ruling sends a message to public school students that the state has a right to invade their bodies *at any time, for any reason* it deems appropriate. Meanwhile, teen violence and drug use continue.

With the noble goal of making the streets safer, the federal government may now, under certain circumstances, search and seize citizens' personal property, including cars, businesses, homes, bank accounts, and personal records without an indictment, hearing, or trial. During a twelve-day period in 1995, police made 2,294 DWI arrests at checkpoints in North Carolina. At these same sobriety checkpoints, police handed out over 34,000 additional violations. Though police supposedly used these checkpoints to look for drunken drivers, they seemed all too eager to search and seize.

The challenge to freedom is the temptation to trade freedom

for a politician's promise of safety from drugs, crime, and terrorism. The pages of history books are filled with examples of abuse resulting from citizens bartering away their liberties to government leaders. As the state acquires more and more power "in the name of protecting its citizens," American government increasingly resembles an intrusive police force wielding the billy clubs of drug tests, curfews, sobriety checkpoints, surveillance cameras, and antiterrorism legislation. The potential for tyranny is so well camouflaged as protection that many Americans fail to recognize the terms of the trade—or the price that we may pay.

THE POINT IS . . .

Pretend for a moment that you have a seven-year-old daughter. One day, a police officer shows up at your door. He says that you've been accused of child abuse. So right there, before your eyes, the policeman takes your little girl.

That can't happen, you say. Well, that's what the Bezette family thought. That is, until one day in May when officers with the Washington County, Utah, Sheriff's Department removed the Bezettes' seven-year-old daughter from their home. For over seventeen hours, officials kept her away from her family. Why? Simply because an anonymous caller accused the Bezettes, a home-schooling family, of child abuse. The caller had no proof. The government officials examining the Bezettes' daughter found no evidence of abuse. Though all charges against the Bezettes were eventually dropped, this family filed some charges of their own. They filed a civil suit claiming their rights as parents, a child, and a family had been violated. But a federal judge dismissed the case. So with help from The Rutherford Institute, the Bezettes appealed their case to the Tenth Circuit Court of Appeals.

The point is that government officials should not be able to take a child from her parents' home simply because of rumors of abuse. This violates the protections of the Fourth and Fourteenth Amendments to our United States Constitution.

THE GOVERNMENT'S "POWER PLAY"

In ice hockey, a "power play" occurs when one team has a man in the penalty box and thus must play shorthanded. If the opposing team takes advantage of the "power play," the result is often a goal.

In life, a power play occurs every time two people interact. Our days, in fact, are filled with power plays. Some are small in scale, as when a store manager refuses to let an employee reschedule a vacation day or a parent forces a child to finish his or her vegetables.

Other power plays occur in larger arenas. A teacher strip-searches his students to look for missing money. A police officer intimidates an innocent man into confessing to a crime. Or a federal agency guns down citizens it deems dangerous "religious fanatics."

Why do people with power abuse it so often? You may be surprised to learn of one person who has thought hard on this question. In a published article, Clint Eastwood wrote about the dangers of power in general and political power in particular.

"Those in power get jaded, deluded and seduced by power itself," he explained. "The hunger for absolute power and, more to the point, the abuse of power, are part of human nature."

It turns out that Eastwood has a lot to say—both on and off the screen—about absolute power. In fact, it's the title of a film that he starred in and directed. Though the film was not pat-terned after any specific government leader, it's difficult to watch without thinking about Watergate, Whitewater, or other politi-cal scandals.

Absolute Power is the story of a jewel thief who witnesses the murder of a woman at the hands of the president of the United States. The president mistakenly thinks his position grants him absolute power, and his loyal Secret Service agents stop at noth-ing to maintain his innocence.

Eastwood says he found himself fascinated by the film's treatment of power—especially within the government. And his skepticism toward the federal government runs deeper than his work as an actor. In *Playboy* magazine, Eastwood "came out" as a libertarian. There, the man best known as Dirty Harry shared the concerns of many Americans and questioned the fed-eral government's handling of Waco and Ruby Ridge in which questionable tactics by federal officers caused the deaths of dozens of citizens.

Yet it was another film—*Waco: The Rules of Engagement*, a documentary released at Robert Redford's Sundance Film Festival—that reignited the fire of controversy burning over the government's role at Waco. In what the *San Francisco Chronicle* dubbed "One of the most disturbing films you'll ever see," *Waco: The Rules of Engagement* claims that federal forces—in contrast to official testimony—fired repeatedly at the Branch Davidians on April 19, 1993. The well-researched documentary, made by former CNN newsman Dan Gifford, his wife Amy, and Mike McNulty, suggests the government may have covered up the true story behind the Waco siege.

In years to come, Waco could find its way into history books, along with Watergate, as an example of the government's abuse of power. This abuse proved fatal at Waco. But the tragedy was a wake-up call to remind America why our Founding Fathers cre-ated a government with *limited* powers—and why Lord Acton warned so aptly, "Power corrupts, and absolute power corrupts absolutely."

THE POINT IS . . .

What do the FBI, the FDA, and the IRS have in common? Each is a powerful arm of our federal government. If you take a look at our Constitution, though, you will not find these federal agencies there. You won't find executive orders, the president's cabinet, the right to die, or the right to have an abortion, either.

No amendments were attached to the Constitution at first. But when it came time for ratification, some state delegates feared the new federal government would be too powerful over the states and the people. They demanded a list of safeguards—a Bill of Rights—to limit the federal government's power. However, some framers pointed out a hidden danger. If any items were left out of the Bill of Rights, the federal government might someday assume it could rule over those areas. That's why they added the Tenth Amendment, which is intended to draw a line around the powers of the federal government.

Despite the Tenth Amendment, however, the federal government has grown into a massive bureaucracy over the past 200 years. Today, it intrudes into nearly every aspect of a citizen's life—from how parents raise their children, to whether prayers may be uttered in public, or whether Bibles may be brought to public schools.

The point is that we must protect our freedoms and learn the lessons of history. If not, we will face an uncertain future.

MILITARIZING MAYBERRY

"To serve and to protect"—that's the motto printed on the doors of police cars from California to Maine. Yet in more and more communities across this country, the police officer's motto is changing. It seems that police officers are being transformed from social workers who keep peace to specialized military officers who elicit fear. Somehow, I don't think Sheriff Andy Taylor would approve.

The policeman's motto, "To serve and to protect," started to fade about the same time that Special Weapons and Tactics, or SWAT, teams stormed on the scene. SWAT teams were first called to action in 1974. Initially, their use was limited to highly specialized activities like hostage situations, but this slowly changed.

As the war on drugs escalated and the violence of gang activities increased, SWAT teams began popping up "to serve and protect" their communities. The number and power of SWAT teams have increased dramatically. Ninety percent of big cities now have active teams, compared with 60 percent in the 1980s.

In a large city like Fresno, California, urban-camouflaged, submachine gun-toting SWAT members now patrol the streets. They routinely carry gas bombs, shields, and semiautomatic weapons that are sold to them by the same private organizations that train their specialized teams. In Fresno, it appears to be the status quo where SWAT teams stand guard to protect and serve.

Most of us don't have SWAT teams traversing the streets of our towns and would be caught off guard if we saw one in our neighborhood. Yet for the most part, Americans have become quite accustomed to viewing SWAT teams on the six o'clock news as they descend upon a bank during a robbery or a workplace where someone is held hostage.

We convince ourselves that SWAT teams have become a necessary evil in this age of violence. Yet as we give these military-like officers more authority to keep our cities, streets, and homes safe, they put down deeper roots in our lives—and begin to become a permanent fixture. Before we know it, their roots start to strangle the once healthy towns, schools, and homes they are supposed to protect.

When a SWAT team descended upon the home of Casey and Stephanie MacDonald, they said they came to serve and protect the MacDonalds' four children. But that couldn't have been further from the truth.

An anonymous caller had telephoned the Bureau of Child Welfare, accusing the MacDonalds of abusing their children. The allegations included claims that the children had bad breath and bad teeth. When the MacDonalds refused to allow the police officers to illegally enter their home and interrogate their children, the government pulled out all the stops to search and seize their children. Social workers—armed with trumped-up accusations of abuse—arrived at their apartment with emergency relief workers, half a dozen police officers, and a full-fledged SWAT team.

Mr. MacDonald refused to give in to the demands of the police *or* the SWAT team. He boldly defended his right as an American citizen to resist unwarranted searches and seizures of his home and his family.

Sound unbelievable? It still does to Casey and Stephanie MacDonald. But it's not. Just ask their children: they will never forget the night the SWAT team tried to take them away from their parents. Now they know there's no such place as Mayberry.

THE POINT IS . . .

In Oklahoma, a bomb devastated a federal building, killing innocent men, women, and children. In Saudi Arabia, a terrorist bombing took the lives of nineteen Americans. And during the 1996 Summer Olympics in Atlanta, a pipe bomb wounded over 100 people, two fatally. Such acts of terrorism leave Americans feeling scared, angry, and, worst of all, helpless. Hoping to gain some sort of power or control, many Americans are tempted to give the government more power. But such a temptation has grave consequences.

Historically, the police force has been a group of civilians who serve their fellow civilians, not an army trained to control by force. Citizens must wonder if their communities really want police officers with the mindset and tactics of the military.

The point is that a system of defense set up against outsiders may one day be used to oppress insiders. So what are we to do about terrorism? There is no easy answer. But we can start by breaking down the barriers that separate families, neighbors, races, and even nations. And we can respond by actively supporting the victims of hate crimes and terrorism.

ON PRIVACY AND RUNNING RED LIGHTS

For many Americans, the simple act of turning on the evening news can be terrifying. We not only have Iraq, Algeria, Bosnia, or some other threat to worry about, but it seems that multitudes of Americans are being harassed in their own workplaces, mugged on the way home, and broadsided by drunk drivers running red lights. It's enough to give anyone a permanent case of insomnia.

In contrast, imagine a perfectly safe world where tragedies like these simply didn't occur—where constant surveillance in the parks prevented drug pushers from approaching your kids, where people drove with caution because hidden cameras would spot violators. No one could harass you at work because video cameras watched every move.

Sound crazy? Actually, this scenario is not as unrealistic as it once seemed. In many states, police are installing cameras to photograph traffic violators in the act. A Manhattan park installed video cameras to cut down on drug pushing. On the job, some employers have video cameras watching every move. In effect, surveillance becomes prevention, and America appears to be moving rapidly in that direction. We essentially expect our government to hire a private bodyguard for each of us.

A few years ago, many would have greeted these changes with alarm, preferring to live with a few more risks in exchange

for more privacy. After all, America is a republic, not a totalitarian state. Our Founding Fathers fought for the right to make our
own personal choices. Privacy is a cherished American tradition,
protected by our Constitution. Why, then, are we casually trading this privacy, step by step, for more intrusion into our lives?

The answer is simple. We don't want a deranged coworker
shooting everyone in sight. The fears we once held concerning
invasion of privacy have given way to other concerns such as personal safety, wealth, and respect. In order to keep our bodies,
wallets, self-esteem, and reputation intact, we're willing to
exchange privacy and personal control over our lives.

Unfortunately, there seems to be a problem here. Many
Americans mistrust the same government they are negotiating
with. Just a few years ago, for example, a TIME/CNN poll indicated that 52 percent of Americans believed "The federal government has become so large and powerful that it poses a threat
to the rights and freedoms of ordinary citizens." In 1995, a joint
survey by Democrats and Republicans discovered that three-
fourths of Americans distrusted the government, responding that
they rarely or never trust "government to do what is right."

These shifting attitudes toward government show that there
are periods when Americans will not be happy with elected officials and may even fear them. (That distrust of "big government"
is even built into our Constitution.) It doesn't make sense, then,
to set up systems of control that can be easily exploited in less
favorable times.

For example, we may not object to cameras catching speed-
ers. But it would be fairly simple for the same equipment to monitor other aspects of your life—whether or not you were wearing
a seatbelt, who your passengers are, what time you *really* left
home. Once a system is in place, an unethical individual (or
group of them) can easily use the same processes for non-
legitimate activities that were not authorized.

In light of this, why set up systems whereby we, the people, can be more strictly monitored by an entity that we cannot completely control? Perhaps we should focus our efforts on justice instead—harsher punishments for people who actually break the law. Perhaps we should work toward improving society's respect for the individual. If changes like this take place in our homes and communities, we won't need Big Brother watching us. And, in the long run, that might be safer than hiring him for a bodyguard.

THE POINT IS . . .

How much force is too much force when police deal with nonviolent offenders? Is it okay for a police officer to Mace a person who is not resisting arrest—even someone who is already handcuffed?

According to a federal appeals court, Macing a handcuffed, nonviolent offender isn't going too far. The court said that when Dallas police officers sprayed pepper Mace in the faces of nonviolent pro-life protesters, they acted within legal boundaries even though the protesters weren't resisting arrest even though these same protesters were already handcuffed. The incident was captured on video, and the police department reprimanded the officers involved. But the court refused to hold them liable for their actions.

The point is that police officers are entitled to use reasonable and necessary force when faced with a violent or dangerous criminal, but spraying pepper Mace in the faces of nonviolent, handcuffed citizens is an outrageous abuse of power. The pro-life protesters were simply trying to follow their religious belief in the sanctity of human life. By sanctioning these acts of police misconduct, this court violated its duty to protect basic constitutional freedoms—and condoned an atmosphere of tyranny.

FREEDOM OF SPEECH

DETECTING POLITICALLY INCORRECT SPEECH

School officials at Montvale Elementary School couldn't believe the magazine that fifth grader Jason Gardner was caught reading. But, in retrospect, they shouldn't have been surprised. After all, Jason had a history of bringing offensive material to school—that is, if you consider Rush Limbaugh's books *offensive.*

In 1995, Jason took Limbaugh's book, *The Way Things Ought to Be,* to school for free reading time. But a teacher was so outraged by this politically incorrect book that it was confiscated. Jason's family responded by filing a lawsuit, which alleged that the school had violated their son's constitutional rights.

While some public school teachers might get weak-kneed at the thought of defending themselves in a lawsuit, the teachers at Montvale Elementary remained steadfast in their determination to continue to censor politically incorrect reading material, a determination matched only by that of Jason Gardner. For Jason refused to be censored. And in 1996, Jason again brought from home what he knew was controversial material. He looked forward to reading it whenever he had some free time at school.

Unlike some fifth grade boys, Jason wasn't cuddling up with the latest issue of a pornographic magazine. His tastes were quite different, and for his reading pleasure, Jason preferred magazines *without* glossy pictures. Selecting something intellectually stimulating, Jason read Rush Limbaugh's *The Limbaugh Letter*. As it turned out, had Jason been reading a pornographic magazine, his actions might have remained undetected.

As soon as Jason began reading *The Limbaugh Letter*, public school teachers confiscated the publication. Yet even though the material had been confiscated, the Montvale teachers still weren't assured their school was safe from such politically incorrect propaganda. So to guarantee that Limbaugh's dangerous materials stayed out of their school, several of the fifth grade teachers implemented a formal policy banning students from bringing recreational reading from home.

Once again, the Gardner family confronted their son's school and asked officials to reverse their policy banning books and magazines that were not part of the Montvale school library. And when the school refused, Jason's parents grew more convinced that they had made the right decision in asking the courts to protect their son's constitutional rights.

Traditionally, our courts have recognized that public schools were intended to be a true marketplace of ideas where young minds could be free to learn, discover, and discern. Legally, public schools cannot censor students' reading materials simply because the materials are *politically incorrect*. Once schools allow students to read books of their own choosing, they cannot subjectively pick and choose which topics or viewpoints they deem acceptable.

Unfortunately, Montvale Elementary School falls far short of being a marketplace of ideas. Instead, it more closely resembles a high security airport, where students must surrender any suspicious material at the gate. As the very ones who allegedly need to be protected from "dangerous ideas," the fifth grade students are no longer free to learn. What the public school teachers don't realize is that the harm has already been done. Be assured, the PC police stand ready to defend their mission: to ensure that only politically correct materials pass through the public school's surveillance system.

THE POINT IS . . .

At what age does a child learn that it's no longer socially acceptable to talk about God in public? Is it at age three, or five, or twelve? Jessica Otto from Elk Grove, California, learned the lesson at age ten. A fifth grader at Foulks Ranch Elementary School, Jessica sang a song about Jesus during her audition for the school talent show. The song raised a few eyebrows during tryouts, which caused the Parent Teachers Association to review a tape of Jessica's performance. PTA officials forbade Jessica from singing her song because of its reference to "Jesus." And to prevent Jesus' name from making it to tryouts in the future, school officials wrote a new policy forbidding religious content in the talent show.

Though she's no stage mom, Jessica's mother jumped in to fight for justice for her child. She called The Rutherford Institute, requesting our legal help. Our attorneys contacted school officials and advised them of Jessica's legal rights. The next day, the superintendent assured The Rutherford Institute that Jessica would be free to sing the song of her choice—a song about Jesus.

The point is that school officials cannot legally censor students' speech simply because of its religious content. Such censorship serves only to chill the free-speech rights of children and incorrectly teaches them that talking about or to God must only be done in private.

TAKING A STAND AT THE POLE

After the soccer championship game, Todd went out to dinner to celebrate, while the rest of his teammates went to a party to get drunk. Saturday night after the football team's victory, Shannon went to a movie with her boyfriend, while some of the other cheerleaders headed to hotel rooms with some of the football team.

Monday morning, long before school started for the day, Deirdre headed to the school's flagpole to pray, while many of her classmates were still at home getting ready for school.

What enables some kids—like Todd, Shannon, and Deirdre—to go against the flow and take a stand, a stand for what they believe in, a stand apart from their peers? Regardless of a teenager's athletic ability, physical appearance, or academic intelligence, unless that person possesses the ability to take a stand for his beliefs and apart from his friends, his life is not his own.

All across this country, kids are doing things they don't want to do, like getting drunk or sleeping around, simply because they don't have the guts to say "No." Likewise, others are avoiding activities they like to do—such as praying or studying—because they don't have the self-confidence to stand apart from their peers.

Rather than face rejection, many young people are willing to throw away their future health, family, and education. Without a thought for their future, they risk an overdose on drugs or alcohol, contraction of the AIDS virus, an unwanted pregnancy, or expulsion from school. They believe that anything's worth the feeling of acceptance, however fleeting it may be.

Few teenagers today have the self-confidence and sense of worth to take a stand for their beliefs. Deirdre is one of the rare exceptions. Deirdre had heard about the annual "See You at the Pole" prayer rallies taking place at schools across the country. She believed her community, teachers, and classmates could benefit from such prayer. So she learned her legal rights about school prayer, gathered support from her local church, and headed to the principal's office.

With the confidence of a seasoned businesswoman, Deirdre informed her principal that she had organized a "See You at the Pole" gathering. She asked permission to advertise the event with posters on campus.

The principal said no, explaining that the prayer rally was "inappropriate" and could not be allowed on campus. Instead of being intimidated by her principal, Deirdre clarified that she wasn't asking permission to hold the "See You at the Pole" gathering, since the right to pray on school property before school hours was legal. Rather, she was simply seeking permission to hang posters.

Again the principal said no. So Deirdre turned to other methods of advertising, relying on personal invitations and word-of-mouth. Most students were not interested. Many who were interested may have been too scared to take a stand for their religious beliefs.

"See You at the Pole" was a small gathering at Windham High School in Windham, Maine. But Deirdre made sure the few hardy souls who did show up felt comfortable as they prayed for the needs of their school.

Deirdre stood up, literally, for her religious beliefs and was willing to face the consequences. Regardless of whether she was taking a stand for prayer at school or abstinence from premarital sex or illegal drugs, what's important is that Deirdre had what it took to stand up for her beliefs, regardless of her peers' actions.

Students such as Deirdre should be held up as leaders because of their courage. Deirdre's teachers should encourage her. Her parents should be proud of her. Her classmates should emulate her. And we should remember her name, for taking a stand is the stuff of which leaders are made.

THE POINT IS . . .

With all the trouble in public schools today, it's hard to imagine why school officials harass students who simply want to read their Bibles. But harass them they do. In 1993, Melanie Ceniceros, a student at University City High School in San Diego, caused quite a stir when she tried to read the Bible with others at lunchtime. Even though other student groups could meet together during lunch, school officials refused to give Melanie's Bible club the same rights. But with the help of a Rutherford Institute attorney, Melanie sued her high school. The court ruled in favor of Melanie, relying on the Equal Access Act's protection of the rights of religious groups. Yet even though the law was clearly on the students' side, the school district refused to accept the court's ruling. It filed for a rehearing. And four years later, the same court voted three to one to affirm its earlier decision, which favored Melanie. Though most of the Bible club's original members have now graduated, it is hoped that University City High School will get the message that the Bible club is here to stay.

The point of law is that the Equal Access Act protects the rights of religious student clubs to meet during noninstructional times at public schools. And the United States Constitution protects the rights of students to free religious expression. Thanks to Melanie, students at University City High and at high schools across the country enjoy greater religious freedom.

CHRISTMAS IN THE CLASSROOM

Do you remember the alphabet circle once painted on kindergarten classroom floors? Perhaps to the classroom designers of past generations, that circle not only provided a more intimate atmosphere for learning but also fostered continuity, inclusion, and identity.

Though the alphabet circle is now absent from most classrooms, public schools have a new approach to promoting feelings of belonging—eliminating all differences among students by silencing them. In this new code of conduct, the golden rule is rewritten to read, "Offend no one." One parent encountered this unspoken censorship when she was invited to lead story time just five days before Christmas.

This was not the mother's first trip to her child's classroom, where parents regularly volunteered to lead story time. Because her turn coincided with the holiday season, she thought the ideal story to tell would be the original Christmas story that began nearly 2,000 years ago. But then she remembered the memo.

Sent weeks earlier, it was a stern reminder by the school principal that children in public schools could not celebrate Christmas. The sensitive kindergarten teacher added in her own handwriting, "It's that old 'separation of church and state' thing."

While the children seemed to enjoy *A Pocket for Corduroy*,

the mother felt a certain injustice in her eventual decision to change her choice of books. There was no reason the children should not have been allowed to hear a story about the first Christmas. But she had given up the fight long ago, when, after generating a few ripples when her first child was going through school, well-meaning family and friends had advised her to be a help, not a hindrance, to her child's education.

Unfortunately, far too many parents, students, and teachers erroneously think they cannot do anything to celebrate Christmas in the public school. Whether it is through ignorance or fear, Americans are painfully misguided about the recognition of religious holidays. Ironically, the most targeted religious holiday for exclusion is Christmas—also the most popular in American culture. Are children to be forbidden from learning about one of the most culturally significant events because it is religious?

There are constitutional ways to celebrate Christmas in school without violating the United States Constitution. While it is true that public school teachers, as agents of the state, may not advance religion, they may discuss the role of religion in all aspects of American culture and its history.

Teachers can use Christmas art, music, literature, and drama in their classrooms, as long as they illustrate the cultural heritage from which the holiday has developed. Religious symbols, like a nativity scene or a cross, can be used in this context as well. Of course, any holiday observance should occur in an educational setting rather than in a devotional atmosphere. Teachers should also remember to offer to students and their parents their district's opt-out policy as an alternative to a teaching about any particular religion.

While our Constitution does not give us *carte blanche* to promote religion in the public schools, neither does it dictate a cleansing of Christmas from the classroom. Students may enjoy the same freedom of religious expression they do any other time of the year—in or out of the classroom.

This means they can freely distribute Christmas or Hanukkah cards to their friends and teachers, just as they would a birthday card. Such cards can even mention the words God and Jesus Christ. Eliminating the differences within our culture does not protect our children from hurt feelings or persecution. It merely renders them ill-informed and afraid, which is the surest way to destroy their freedom.

THE POINT IS . . .

I'm not sure what the fascination is with having your face painted, but children sure seem to love it. Whenever a community fair or open house advertises free face painting, a line of children seems to form instantaneously. Restless children seem to have no trouble sitting still as a train or a clown is painted on their cheek.

So when the Martinsburg, West Virginia, local Parent Teacher Association announced their annual Fall Festival, face painters began to line up. Pastor Ken Burkhart wanted to join in on the action by bringing his Child Evangelism Fellowship face painters to man a booth. But the PTA turned down his request—even though they had already accepted two other face-painting applicants. Their reason: the face painters with Child Evangelism Fellowship told Bible stories as they painted. The PTA feared that the Bible stories violated the so-called "separation of church and state."

After hearing about this incident, The Rutherford Institute wrote to Pastor Burkhart, explaining his legal right to free expression. After the pastor showed the PTA a copy of our letter, fair organizers agreed to let the Christian face painters man a booth at the fair.

The point of law is religious censorship. The PTA cannot discriminate against a group based upon the content of that group's speech—even if that speech is unpopular or religious in nature.

ALIENS AND EVOLUTION

Moviegoers who saw the 1997 film *Contact* found themselves enthralled by the immensity and beauty of the universe. In a dramatic opening, director Robert Zemeckis zoomed the viewers away from the Earth, beyond the Milky Way, into the depths of distant space. The story that follows leaves viewers pondering questions about the relationships of scientific inquiry, the existence of God, and alien life. Does science oppose faith?

While a film such as *Contact* may raise such questions for a willing audience, millions of unsuspecting schoolchildren have this question posed to them every year in their science classes when they encounter the theory of evolution.

Religious parents have often protested the teaching of the theory of evolution in the public schools, and rightly so. With the publication of the book that began the evolution movement, Charles Darwin's *Origin of Species* in 1859, much of the foundations of Jewish and Christian religious belief began to disintegrate. Darwin's theory denies the worth and dignity formerly attributed to people created in God's image, and it relegates human beings to the realm of the animal world.

Far from being presented as another hypothesis, evolution has the distinction of frequently being taught as fact, although there is good scientific evidence that the theory as we have it today may not be as factual as it claims to be. For religious students who believe God created the world, some of the tenets of evolution seem more like atheism than science, and that view may well destroy a child's faith in his/her parents, organized religion, and God.

Most public schools blatantly disregard these legitimate concerns—a fact that is distressing to many religious parents. However, in one unusual case handled by The Rutherford Institute, a school board in Louisiana adopted a resolution to have instructors read a disclaimer to students before presenting the theory of evolution. The disclaimer read:

> It is hereby recognized . . . that the lesson to be presented, regarding the origin of life and matter, is known as the Scientific Theory of Evolution and should be presented to inform students of the scientific concept and not intended to influence or dissuade the Biblical version of Creation or any other concept.
>
> It is further recognized . . . that it is the basic right and privilege of each student to form his/her own opinion or maintain beliefs taught by parents on this very important matter of the origin of life and matter. Students are urged to exercise critical thinking and gather all information possible and closely examine each alternative toward forming an opinion.

Although the school refused to present Creation Science as an alternative in class, it did attempt to provide a reasonable response to the concerns of the parents of their diverse student body. The disclaimer did not advance any religion and simply acknowledged the existence of diverse viewpoints.

Amazingly, a few local parents, with the help of the ACLU, filed suit, claiming that the disclaimer jeopardized their children's right to a religion-free public education. Their rights to a religion-free education? It hardly seems that allowing a student to make his or her own decisions with the guidance of parents is imposing religion on anyone. Rather than allowing the views of the many religious students even to be acknowledged, the ACLU is trying to stifle the slightest nod of accommodation to religious persons.

The First Amendment was created to protect the rights of religious persons—not smother them. With this case, *Freiler v. Tangipahoa Parish Board of Education*, the ACLU is attempting to destroy the right of religious schoolchildren to be aware that the material being presented may be at odds with the teaching of the parents and that it may also be false. Adults may benefit from the questions posed by *Contact*, as they discern the differences between reality and fiction, science and speculation. Children, however, need more guidance than this movie—or a typical public education science textbook—provides.

THE POINT IS . . .

Adam and Eve. Everybody knows who they are. But how many people actually believe that they really existed, that they lived in the Garden of Eden, and that the entire human race descended from them? Thanks to recent reports from geneticists, a lot more people are Adam and Eve believers.

It all started about eight years ago, when genetic researchers concluded that all modern humans descended from a single, though theoretical, woman. They named her "Mitochondrial Eve," after the part of the cell that transfers from mother to child. Well, now scientists have surprised themselves again. Two recent reports in Nature magazine claim that all modern men share genes from one male ancestor. The male ancestor was appropriately named "Y-chromosome Adam."

This so-called discovery of Mitochondrial Eve and Y-chromosome Adam has rocked the world of secularists. For starters, it shoots holes in their theory that humans emerged independently, in different places, across different continents. Genetic Adam and Eve confirm that mankind originated in a specific geographic location and multiplied from there.

The point is that genetic research is confirming what people of faith have believed for thousands of years: there really was an Adam and an Eve. And all people have descended from them. It's probably only a matter of time before botanists realize that there really was a Garden of Eden as well.

GRANDSTANDING FOR FREE SPEECH

If you're a Cincinnati Reds baseball fan, then you've probably heard of Guy Aubrey. Even if you're not, if you watched the 1990 World Series when the Reds played the Oakland Athletics, you may have caught a glimpse of Aubrey on your television screen.

Aubrey's no relief pitcher, pinch hitter, or third base coach. Guy Aubrey is "The John 3:16 Guy." Certainly, you've seen his work. While most fans are listening to the crack of the bat and watching the players on the field, Guy Aubrey's concern is directed toward the souls of the thousands of baseball fans around him. His official title is *Reverend* Guy Aubrey, and his game plan is to share the message of John 3:16 with those in the grandstand.

But Aubrey's strategy didn't go over well with the Reds' management. When Aubrey attempted to display his "John 3:16" banner during Game Two of the World Series, he was told that his sign violated a policy banning religious signs and banners. The sign was confiscated, but Aubrey wasn't out of the game yet.

Reverend Aubrey took the Reds to court, arguing that his religious speech—in this case a religious banner—deserved as much protection as other forms of speech, such as the "Just say 'No' to drugs" T-shirt worn by the man who sat next to him in the stands. Free speech is free speech.

The court apparently agreed and found that the Reds' policy

of banning religious banners was vague and overbroad. The Reds had violated Aubrey's freedom of speech.

Instead of relaxing their rules and allowing free speech to reign, however, the Reds responded to the court's ruling by laying down a new, even more restrictive law. Rather than opening up the stadium to all types of speech, the Reds decided that only "baseball-related" signs were allowed in the stadium.

Aubrey complied and brought a sign that read, "Go Reds—John 3:16" to fit the regulations. Once again, the Reds forced him to surrender his sign. And once again, the reverend called "interference" and took the team to court. This time, a federal court found the Reds' restrictive sign policy unconstitutional.

Eventually, the Reds decided to abide by the rules and rewrote their policy to allow fans to display signs—even "John 3:16"—without discrimination. At last, there was a victory for free speech.

The Reds and the City of Cincinnati even agreed to award Guy Aubrey a $20,000 settlement. Instead of putting the money toward tickets for the next baseball season, Guy Aubrey gave it away. Donated to a church in Chihuahua, Mexico, the $20,000 was used to buy land for a new sanctuary.

Guy Aubrey wasn't grandstanding for his fifteen seconds of fame or to make a fortune. He simply wanted to exercise his freedom of speech while enjoying a day at the ballpark. And when you think about it, freedom of speech is about as American as baseball and apple pie. Reverend Guy Aubrey wanted to make sure it stays that way.

THE POINT IS . . .

Do you remember the runner Jim Ryun? In the 1972 Olympics in Munich, Ryun was America's hope for a gold medal in the 1500-meter race. But that hope came to an abrupt end when, just 500 meters short of the finish line in his qualifying race, Jim fell. But he didn't stay down for long. He turned his Olympic tragedy into a lifelong triumph of encouraging others, especially our youth, to turn to God in trying times. Jim spends a great deal of time traveling nationwide sharing his life story about his sport and his faith.

Recently, before giving a speech in a high school in Kansas, Jim was told that he couldn't talk about God. Since Jim listens to "Freedom under Fire," he knew his rights were being violated and gave The Rutherford Institute a call for help. That same day, we faxed a letter explaining Jim's legal rights. The event went off without interference because, with the help of The Rutherford Institute, Jim Ryun stood up for both his faith and his rights.

The point is that to make Jim Ryun talk about running without talking about God is not only impossible—it's also illegal. If a public school opens its doors to outside speakers, it cannot censor speeches that mention God. When given a hurdle of religious discrimination, Jim Ryun showed the same determination and grace that helped make him a world-class runner.

UP AGAINST
THE WALL

In 1803, when Thomas Jefferson coined the phrase "the wall of separation between church and state," he envisioned an invisible wall that would protect the church from unnecessary intrusion by the state—not promote it.

Though this phrase is found nowhere in the United States Constitution, government agencies have all but institutionalized the "wall." State employees are often expected to shed their beliefs when they clock in for work and can face stern discipline if they refuse. Some instances of unacceptable behavior include placing a Bible on one's desk or sharing religious convictions with a coworker.

Monte Tucker is one example of a government employee who refused to leave his religious beliefs at the office door. As a California state employee, Monte first hit the "wall" when he designed a computer screen that displayed a clever acronym—"SLJC." The letters stood for "servant of the Lord Jesus Christ." Never expecting to elicit any animosity by this silent expression, Tucker had devised the words as a personal reminder of his deeply-held religious beliefs.

But Tucker's acronym reminded his supervisor of the "wall." The boss issued an ultimatum to Tucker: either remove the religious acronym or face suspension from his job. Religious expression was not allowed for state employees in California.

Initially, Tucker refused to remove "SLJC." Then a new department policy was implemented: employees were forbidden from sharing their faith and displaying or storing any personal religious items, like Bibles, except in closed offices. Since there were no closed offices in Monte's workplace, only cubicles, the new policy effectively forbade any personal religious expression. He was then forced to question if maybe this wall was too tough to scale by himself. But his religious beliefs were too sacred for him not to try, so he refused to comply with the new policy.

A lawsuit followed, filed on Monte Tucker's behalf in federal district court by The Rutherford Institute. The court didn't see a problem with the State of California restricting its employees' religious expression in the workplace. The next step was the Ninth Circuit Court of Appeals. The Rutherford Institute asked the court to scrutinize the policy and overturn the district court's decision. Investigating the circumstances more thoroughly, the appeals court ruled in Monte's favor and declared the state's policy unconstitutional.

Rutherford Institute attorneys applauded the appeals court decision, saying, "This is an important victory for government workers' right to individual religious expression in the workplace. The California Department of Education will no longer be able to engage in religious sterilization of the workplace. Further, this case will serve as a valuable precedent to challenge similar antireligious government policies across the country."

Sadly, there are too many antireligious policies in the workplace. In today's America, while the church is held firmly at bay behind Jefferson's "wall," the state often breaches it to interfere with individual religious expression. Jefferson's phrase was intended to *protect* the religious expression of the people—even those, like Monte Tucker, who work on the state's side of the wall.

THE POINT IS . . .

If you wanted to express your religious beliefs on your license plate, what would you say? Patricia Wall of Dandridge, Tennessee, chose the phrase "God 4 U." But Tennessee's Department of Safety threw a glitch in her plan. According to Supervisor Karen Edwards, the computer at Tennessee's Department of Safety was programmed to deny any license plate with the word God in it. They said it was "the computer" that denied Patricia's request for a "God 4 U" plate. Well, The Rutherford Institute sent what's referred to as a "legal demand letter" to officials at the Tennessee Department of Safety. They were very responsive to our concerns. Recently we were told that Patricia's request for a "God 4 U" license plate has now been approved—along with an apology for any inconvenience and misunderstanding caused by the mix-up. State officials blamed the initial rejection on a "computer error" and promised to update the computer to accept God's name in the future.

The point of law is viewpoint discrimination. It's unconstitutional to deny license plate tags simply because they contain a religious word or phrase. It is inexcusable for state officials to program a computer to selectively censor the name of God from all Tennessee license plates. Does your state censor God's name from your community? Take a look around and see what types of discrimination you see.

TAKE THIS JOB . . .

Connie McGettigan could have just given up. It would have been easier on everyone—especially on her. She could have just done what her boss wanted or mentally checked out and simply let her body go through the motions. She could have acted like she really didn't care.

But Connie McGettigan did care. She had certain values and beliefs that she simply wasn't willing to ignore, compromise, or change, regardless of what was at stake—even if it meant losing her job. And, this time around, it did.

Connie had worked at L. L. Staffing Services in Chester County, Pennsylvania, for about a year. During that year, Connie received an excellent job performance rating. Her reputation was spotless, except for one detail.

Time and again, Connie had voiced objections to being forced to attend half-day and day-long "values" workshops. I'm sure you know the ones. The company hires an expensive consultant to promote the latest politically correct ideas sweeping through the business world.

The problem was that the values being promoted by L. L. Staffing Services weren't simply about the company's commitment to tolerance, community service, or diversity. Rather, L. L. Staffing Services required Connie to attend values workshops that specifically promoted a New Age religious worldview, a worldview fundamentally at odds with Connie's deeply-held religious beliefs.

To make matters worse, Connie wasn't just required to attend the New Age workshops. Even though her employer knew the seminars violated Connie's religious beliefs, the company forced her to communicate the New Age teachings to the employees under her supervision.

Connie had a decision to make. Should she continue expressing her objections to the New Age seminars? Or should she take the easy way out and pretend the mandatory seminars didn't bother her? She could also give in to her concerns and quit.

But Connie never had to decide. She was fired. After her termination, Connie filed an employment discrimination lawsuit against her former employer. The lawsuit argued that L. L. Staffing Services violated her First Amendment right to religious freedom. It also accused the company of employee discrimination.

To settle the case, a local court ordered mediation hearings. But suspecting that the hearings were headed in Connie's favor, the company rapidly pursued a settlement agreement, a component of which required L. L. Staffing Services to write Connie a favorable letter of recommendation.

Connie was vindicated. But was it worth it? Should she have simply kept her mouth shut, checked her beliefs at the office door, and spouted the party line? Connie doesn't think so. After all, a religious belief isn't worth much if it's not worth fighting for or if it can be given up at the slightest hint of opposition.

Who really cares what happened to Connie McGettigan? Everyone has employment gripes. But if the First Amendment fails to protect Connie's right to possess personal religious beliefs, sooner or later it will fail to protect your right to believe, do, or say something that is dear to you.

If we don't insist on exercising our constitutionally-protected rights to speak and worship freely—like Connie did—in the near future, we may discover that we've lost them for good.

THE POINT IS . . .

Do your religious beliefs ever clash with your job description? Maybe you're a public school teacher directed to plan the Halloween party. Or perhaps you manage a bookstore that sells pornographic magazines. Or maybe, like Calvin Wright, you work for a health insurance company that covers abortions.

Calvin ran into trouble with his company, MetraHealth, when he had to process reimbursements for the costs of abortions. It had been easy to issue payments for throat cultures, x-rays, and hip replacements. But to Calvin, abortions were an entirely different matter. Calvin tried to handle the situation as professionally as he could. He told his company that because of his religious beliefs, he simply could not issue payments on abortions. Their response: "Pay for them or you'll be fired." He was fired.

Calvin contacted The Rutherford Institute to see if he could get his job back. We sent him information on religious accommodation in the workplace and found a lawyer to represent him. As it turned out, the educational material convinced his employer, and our lawyer wasn't needed. MetraHealth reinstated Calvin with back pay. They also adopted a new policy that accommodates anyone with religious objections to abortion.

The point is accommodation. Employers are required to reasonably accommodate the religious beliefs of their employees.

THE SUPREME COURT AND THE IRON CURTAIN: A CRITICAL CASE TESTS DEMOCRACY AS WE KNOW IT

Behind the Iron Curtain, in the former Communist bloc, governments would occasionally sponsor so-called "democratic" elections. When the people arrived at the polling stations, however, only one candidate would appear on the ballot—the official party choice.

This mockery of true democracy seems unthinkable in our country. But it is a scenario heard by the United States Supreme Court with an unfortunate result.

In 1992, Arkansas Educational Television Network, a government-owned station, hosted debates between Arkansas congressional candidates, including those vying for the Third District seat. "Do you know your candidates?" AETN asked in its advertising campaign.

Yet AETN didn't actually introduce Arkansas voters to *all* of their candidates—just those from the Democratic and Republican parties. Another officially-balloted Third District candidate, Ralph Forbes, was excluded from the televised debate.

Forbes was no stranger to the Arkansas political scene. In 1990, he snared 46 percent of the vote in a three-way Republican primary for the lieutenant governor nomination. In that race, he garnered a majority of the vote in fifteen of the sixteen counties comprising the Third District where, in 1992, he was seeking the congressional seat.

Forbes qualified as an official candidate in the 1992 congressional race by acquiring thousands of signatures from registered voters in the Third District. Two months before the debate was scheduled to air, he wrote AETN, asking to be included. The network turned him down. Then, on the night the debate aired, October 22, 1992, he came to the television station in person and requested to participate. Once again, AETN officials refused. In addition, an AETN employee instructed other news reporters covering the debate to ignore Forbes.

Forbes's next step was to contact The Rutherford Institute, which filed suit on his behalf, charging AETN with violating Forbes's First Amendment rights.

In court testimony, AETN executives justified their decision, saying they did not consider Forbes "a viable candidate." Considering Forbes' performance in his 1990 pursuit of the lieutenant governor nomination, AETN's assertion is suspect. But more importantly, Forbes's popularity with the voters was not at issue. As a government entity, AETN's responsibility lay in providing a forum for all balloted candidates, regardless of their chances of victory.

But AETN's arrogance goes even further. The network argued in court documents that, since it is a media outlet, it was the one that deserved First Amendment protection, not Forbes.

A federal district court, the first step on the judicial ladder, agreed with AETN. The Rutherford Institute appealed this decision to the Eighth Circuit Court of Appeals on Forbes's behalf. The Eighth Circuit reversed the lower court's decision, ruling that a subjective evaluation of a candidate's political "viability" is not a legitimate reason for a government entity to ban an officially-balloted candidate. The court chastised AETN for its arbitrary ban of Forbes, stating, "We do not think that [the station's] opinion on such a debatable matter as the political viability of a candidate for Congress more than two months in advance of the election can be a sufficient basis for narrowing the channels of public discourse."

After this setback, AETN's lawyers appealed the case to the Supreme Court.

The Rutherford Institute argued that AETN—as a government actor—has a First Amendment obligation to allow all citizens to participate in the political process.

Unfortunately, the Supreme Court ruled in AETN's favor. The implications of this decision could be ominous and far-reaching. The First Amendment has functioned as a tool to protect the people from the government. The ruling in AETN's favor, though, has essentially flipped the First Amendment on its head. For the first time, it is being used to protect the *government* from the *people*. Such a drastic reinterpretation of the First Amendment could be devastating for civil liberties.

THE POINT IS . . .

The military is always looking for a few good men, or women. That is, as long as they aren't too religious. Or at least that's what Lieutenant Jeannine Ball discovered. While stationed at the Dover Air Force Base, one of Ball's colleagues asked her questions about her faith. Ball responded by giving her coworker copies of a daily devotional. And while this sounds like a perfectly normal response, apparently it wasn't quite kosher with the military. The coworker accused Lieutenant Ball of anti-Semitism and reported her to military authorities. Ball received an incident write-up, which remains part of her permanent file. It also plays an important role in determining promotions. The write-up stated that Ball should keep "all religious quotes, thoughts verbalized, and memento—giving outside this facility, while in uniform and on duty." It went on to warn that she should "not discuss her religion to anyone, whether they are an interested party or not."

After receiving this letter, Lieutenant Ball contacted The

Rutherford Institute. Within hours, our legal staff provided her with material highlighting her legal rights. Ball took our letter and marched directly to her supervisor, who quickly cleared Ball of any wrongdoing.

The point is freedom of speech. Though the military is able to place limits on some forms of expression and speech, they are not able to place blanket restrictions on religious freedom.

INDIVIDUALS
AND FAMILIES

WHEN ABSTINENCE FAILS

No one can question that abstinence reigns unchallenged as the number one way to prevent unwanted pregnancies. But how do proponents of abstinence respond when teens fail to "Just say 'No'"? Do they stone the sexually promiscuous offenders? Brand the adulterers with scarlet letter "A's"? Or silently shun the undesirables who "ruined their lives"?

Perhaps we might look to the community in Franklin Lakes, New Jersey, an affluent suburb of New York City, where then eighteen-year-old Amy Grossman's newborn baby was found bludgeoned to death in a motel dumpster. Was this action the result of perceived responses from other parents and community members to unplanned pregnancies of the past? If that is the case, we can only guess they would have been less than supportive.

If there is ever a time when a girl needs the love, support, and wise counsel of her community, and especially her parents, it's when an unplanned pregnancy occurs. Unfortunately, far too many parents, caught up in their own sense of disappointment, guilt, and failure, react negatively to their daughters upon hearing those dreaded words, "Mom, Dad, I'm pregnant."

When abstinence fails, there's a better way to respond than a trip to the nearest abortion clinic. A response that includes instead of alienates; forgives instead of punishes.

Such compassion can move your pregnant daughter on toward her future instead of drowning in past mistakes. If abstinence fails in your family, here are some ingredients for a better response.

Confront the crisis head-on. Acknowledge your daughter's lack of judgment, then wipe her slate clean. Without this liberating forgiveness, your family will not get past the pregnancy. Move on. Neither your daughter's life, nor your own, is over. A new one is beginning. Pray with your daughter and seek God's guidance. Assure her she has a future, and give her a sense of direction. Respect your daughter. Enable her to make wise decisions about her pregnancy. It is critical for her to understand that her adult behavior now requires adult decisions about her child's future.

Don't hesitate to seek help from the community. A pastor or family counselor can act as a sounding board or referee as the entire family adjusts to the pregnancy and considers financial, educational, and living arrangements for the future. Network, like you would in any other crisis situation. Join your daughter in identifying resources that will help her in the months and years ahead. Contact your local crisis pregnancy center and accompany her on her appointments. There staff members can give her information about proper prenatal care, what to expect during labor and delivery, and provide clothing and equipment to help ease the financial strain. If adoption is a possibility, then agencies supportive of childbirth can identify options and outline the legal rights of the biological mother.

As your daughter looks toward the future, encourage and enable her to complete her education during and after her pregnancy. Juggling school and parenting responsibilities take their toll, so be prepared to provide real help, like child care or baby-sitting money. And though your instincts may scream otherwise, if there is a steady boyfriend involved, include him in decision-making. He is now a father. He needs to start acting like one. And though abstinence failed on at least one occasion, encourage abstinence now. It's never too late to start acting responsibly.

The challenge, when abstinence fails, is to respond with love, support, and compassion. Though teaching abstinence is still the most effective means of preventing pregnancy, the reality is that every teen won't "Just say 'No.'" Rather than putting on the mantle of safe sex, reach out to your daughter and to other single mothers who find themselves in a predicament. If we truly value life, we must consistently do so—even when the failure may be our own.

THE POINT IS . . .

How well do you know your neighbors? Does your relationship consist of saying hello to each other as you get your mail? Or are you involved in each other's lives—sharing meals, doing yard work together, and keeping an eye on each other's children?

Sadly, more and more children are raised in neighborhoods marked by isolation—devoid of a sense of community. Children hop off the school bus in the afternoon and head straight home, making sure not to talk to any strangers along the way. Once they've unlocked their front doors, they lock themselves in their houses waiting in front of the television or computer until their parents arrive home for dinner. This afternoon of isolation repeats itself five days a week, throughout the school year. But it wasn't always this way. Not so long ago, children rushed home from school, dropped their book bags on the sidewalk, and played kickball with their neighbors. The children's mothers or some other relatives were accessible, always within arm's reach. But neighborhoods marked by a sense of community are rare these days. Neighborhoods have changed—in large part because families have changed.

The point is that the responsibility to raise children has shifted away from the family and to others, such as schools, day care centers, and state institutions. As parents, we must recognize our responsibility to our children—and seek to rear them in an atmosphere marked by community, belonging, and most of all, families.

PREDATORS IN CYBERSPACE— A THREE-PRONGED APPROACH

Like many parents, the increasing number of news reports about pedophiles on the Internet troubles me. They're a parent's worst nightmare and usually provoke a flood of arguments about free speech, censorship, and protecting innocent children from wandering into dangerous cyberspace. In response, libraries debate whether or not to limit children's computer access, and FBI personnel disguised as teenagers venture onto the Web to trap molesters.

In this day and age, it's tough for parents to know how to protect their children. They used to think that children were safe in their own home, but now a molester can reach through cyberspace and touch them even in the safety of their own living room. What can a parent do?

I believe that a three-pronged approach is the best solution to the problem—offense, defense, and prevention.

In the realm of offense comes the role of law. While the legalities of censorship may still be debated for a long time to come, the illegality of child pornography and child molestation is still clear. Parents can actively support legislation to toughen penalties for criminals who are caught and encourage their representatives to make sure they're enforced. Some of the most influential people in the legal arena have been family members who tackled issues such as gun control, drunk driving, and kidnapping after they had personal experiences with the crime.

Defensive measures, on the other hand, are mostly enforced in the home. This involves teaching children "Internet safety"— basic things like not releasing their real names or home phone numbers to people they meet on-line. To protect naive youngsters from wandering into dubious websites, a variety of screening software has come onto the market. In the end, the best security is to have a parent monitoring a child's usage. Just have the computer in an easily accessible space, like the living room or den, where Mom or Dad can keep an eye on what the children are looking at. These same rules apply to library usage—go there with your children, help them with their research, and use the opportunity to instruct them about safe surfing.

Prevention, rather than focusing on laws or software, is accomplished by meeting the emotional needs of the children. As I've read the accounts of some of the molesters who found children through the "Net," it seemed odd to me how many children willingly agreed to meet the stranger. Some arranged a clandestine meeting at the mall, while others climbed into cars and actually went to the molester's home or to a hotel room. Something is wrong here!

As any parent will tell you, every child is unique. And their reasons for engaging in risky encounters with strangers will vary. Some teenagers may just be looking for an opportunity to rebel. Others want a taste of danger. Some of the saddest cases, though, are those of children who were so desperate for affection that they looked for it in unsafe places.

A variety of research has been recently released, showing the influence that parents have on their children. For example, the National Institute of Mental Health reports that 90 percent of children from unstable homes become delinquents, compared with only 6 percent from stable homes. And the U.S. Department of Education found that children received higher grades and were less likely to be expelled when their fathers were involved in their schooling.

In light of statistics like this, I wouldn't be surprised to discover that a large percentage of Internet victims came from homes where the parents were not heavily interested in and involved with their children.

In our search for solutions, we miss the point when we focus just on censorship, screening, and more laws. America's children need deeper solutions to the real problems that send them into the arms of strangers.

THE POINT IS . . .

You know that pornography is dangerous. But do you know the dangers it poses for your family? Even families who try their best to shelter themselves from the destructive influence of pornography can't help but be affected, however indirectly, by the increasing power of the porn industry. Just listen to some of the facts, according to a report in U.S. News & World Report: *In 1996, American citizens spent more than eight billion dollars on hardcore videos, peep shows, sex magazines, and other forms of pornography. This is more money than Americans spent at the movies. But do you know who's cashing in on the profits in this growing porn industry? Mom and pop video stores, long-distance phone carriers, and cable companies. Even major hotel chains reported that, in 1996, guests spent some $175 million to view porn in their rooms. It is also estimated that Americans spent nearly one billion dollars on "telephone sex" the same year.*

Pornography's tentacles have a wide reach. And pornography erodes the basic foundations of our society. That's why it's not enough just to hide from it. Instead, we need to come up with a comprehensive plan to pry American families away from pornography's grip before our families are too weak to fight back.

VIOLENCE AND DATING: HOW CAN PARENTS PROTECT THEIR CHILDREN?

What a cute couple the pair made. Eager for approval and affection, "Ginger" never mentioned their fights, the slapping, and "Tim's" increasing control over the little things—how she wore her hair, who she could talk to. No one suspected abuse—until Ginger landed in the hospital.

"Amy" came from a tough home life. Her father drank, pushed her mother around, and even punched Amy once in a while. Amy expected her boyfriend to act the same way, so she wasn't surprised when he slapped and beat her. After all, the next day he usually brought her something nice and made her feel special.

During Domestic Violence Awareness Month in October, women's advocacy groups across the nation hold candlelight vigils, rallies, and art displays to commemorate women who have been injured or killed by an intimate partner. Although much violence occurs within families or cohabiting couples, both physical and emotional abuse are also becoming increasingly common in dating relationships. According to one report, up to one-third of teenaged girls have reported being involved in at least one dating relationship that involved physical abuse—a statistic that strikes fear into the heart of any concerned parent.

What can parents do to safeguard their daughters from an abusive dating relationship? While no parents can completely safeguard their child, the stage for good dating relationships can be set early in life by building close, trusting family relationships. Good communication begins when children are young. It takes effort, time, planning, and imagination on the part of parents. It means reading aloud to your children, playing with them, working with them, and listening to their joys and pains. A girl's relationship with her father will have special impact on her choice of a boyfriend later in life.

It isn't an easy task, but children who grow up in secure families have a strong sense of security, stability, and confidence. A young woman with these traits is less susceptible to abusive relationships. When she has fears or questions, she feels comfortable approaching her parents. An alienated child is a vulnerable child—one who becomes a vulnerable teen.

Children also need good role models to consistently demonstrate how men and women should treat each other. Studies have shown that over half of the children whose parents abused each other have subsequently been involved in abusive dating relationships themselves.

In addition, children need standards. The "house rules" for a six-year-old will differ from those of a sixteen-year-old, of course, but a girl who learns to obey Mom at age six is far more likely to listen at age sixteen. As their child grows, parents should explain the reasons for the rules.

Before the daughter begins to date, her parents should set dating standards. For example, they may require prior approval (including a meeting between the parents and young man) before any date. Another good policy is a curfew for her protection. Parents ought to know where the date will be, how long it will last, etc. If plans change, the daughter can call home. As she gets older and more experienced, the rules can be adjusted accordingly.

Finally, parents should simply be alert for signs of abuse. Even a normally confident young woman may be embarrassed, afraid, or too naive to admit a problem. Domestic Violence Awareness Month reminds us that violence can hit close to home. Alert and loving parents should take this opportunity to consider what they can do to prevent their child—male or female—from becoming a victim (or a perpetrator) of domestic violence.

THE POINT IS . . .

Take a bunch of "Kids with no hope, no fear, no rules, and no life expectancy" and what do you get? A recipe for an explosion of juvenile crime. And that is exactly what John Firman of the International Association of Chiefs of Police reports that officers are increasingly encountering.

According to a U.S. News & World Report *article, the number of children under eighteen years of age arrested for murder tripled between 1984 and 1994. A sixteen-year-old killed a woman for criticizing his rap music. In rural Ohio, two boys, ages six and ten, killed a two-and-a-half-year-old girl. And a pregnant fifteen-year-old was shot to death on a school bus in St. Louis. Experts say things will get worse before they get better, predicting a 25-percent increase in juvenile murder by the year 2005.*

With hopes of a political solution, Americans are turning to their Congresspersons and Senators, demanding action. While conservatives lobby for tougher laws that try violent offenders as adults, liberals fight for increased spending on preventive measures and rehabilitation programs.

The point is that far too many children have "no hope, no fear, no rules, and no life expectancy"—and that is the REAL crime. Our society, our churches, and our families are failing children. It's time we got involved in helping our children because we are all going to pay the price if we don't.

ANTS
IN HIS PANTS

It's a good thing I wasn't born in the 1990s. There's no doubt I would have been put on Ritalin or ended up in juvenile court. I wasn't really abnormal. Simply put, I was a normal boy.

I had a lot of energy—the kind that exhausts mothers and exasperates teachers long before lunchtime arrives. I had trouble concentrating on schoolwork and couldn't sit still for more than a couple of minutes at a time—unless, of course, I was at the movie theater after school. Often, I kept to myself and shied away from playing with other kids.

My mom and my teachers never gave my actions and attitudes much thought. They didn't develop theories about me, blame themselves for my introverted nature, or wonder why I refused to do my homework. No, to them I was normal. A son. A student. A boy. Just like I was supposed to be.

But today, our expectations of boyhood have changed and, I'm afraid, for the worse. Boys who are feisty and energetic—or simply bored—are routinely labeled as having a medical disorder and commonly treated with prescription drugs.

The number of children classified as disabled has skyrocketed over the past several decades. According to a May 2, 1997, issue of *The Wall Street Journal*, a record 5.4 million children are now identified as disabled. This is nearly 25 percent more than ten

years ago. Attention Deficit Disorder or ADD is the fastest-grow-
ing disorder. And boys comprise 80 to 90 percent of ADD cases.

Though I'm no expert, I'm guessing that most boys haven't
changed biologically in the past fifty years. What has changed is
society—and the attitudes of parents, educators, and physicians
toward childhood.

In today's busy world, many parents don't give their children
time to simply be kids. Maybe no one ever told these parents that
little boys need to spend hours a day playing—climbing trees,
fighting wars, and capturing bad guys.

To make matters worse, educators often lack the training or
resources to handle students who don't fit into the system.
Apparently some teachers and administrators are so overworked
that they'd rather have zombies in class instead of normal, fidg-
eting kids.

And physicians often don't have the will to resist the pres-
sures of desperate mothers and fathers seeking a medical solution
to the frustrations of child rearing.

As a society, we stand guilty of robbing boys of their childhood—and we know it. The mother tentatively handing her boy
Ritalin each morning misses the rambunctious son she once
knew. The teacher treating her students like robots notices their
zeal and creativity have disappeared. And the doctor writing out
a prescription suspects that drugs won't solve the family's troubles—they merely put a bandage on them.

Regardless of the excuses, we are guilty of vilifying boyhood.
If we don't wake up and take a good look at our actions, our sons
will pay the price.

THE POINT IS . . .

*When it comes to public education, what is America's number one con-
cern? The answer may surprise you. It's not reading, writing, or arith-
metic. According to a recent Gallup poll, "lack of discipline" is the*

biggest concern of most Americans. And financial concerns and violence closely follow discipline. The poll also found that of those surveyed, over half wanted the federal government less involved in the public schools. And over two-thirds of those surveyed supported a constitutional amendment allowing school prayer. Most preferred a moment of silence.

But perhaps what is most interesting about this Gallup poll are the opinions of those within the public schools. Teachers and students were the least likely to characterize discipline as the top problem of public schools. Instead, teachers and students expressed a growing concern over the lack of parental support.

The point is that the public wants America's public schools—not parents—to shoulder the burden of discipline. And this is a tragic mistake. Many parents have ignored their responsibility to discipline their children. The problem is that the public school system has neither the right nor the ability to serve as the primary disciplinarian to our children. So, parents out there, it's time to wake up and assume your rightful responsibility.

PUBLIC SCHOOL TEACHERS IN PRIVATE SCHOOLS

Should students who attend private schools have access to the benefits of public education—like public school athletic teams, libraries, and special education classes?

Some people view public education as an all or nothing decision. You are either in or out. In fact, these public school supporters become annoyed and angry at parents who opt their children out of public school, yet still want the freedom to take advantage of public education programs. I've learned that when it comes to education, most parents divide into two camps, with very few being brave enough to wander between the two.

Ask parents who send their children to public school if private school kids should have access to public school perks, and their answer is usually predictable: "No way. After all," these public school supporters argue, "private school students opted out of the public school system. They shouldn't be able to pick and choose which programs to take advantage of."

But ask a group of parents who send their children to private school this same question, and they'll usually respond with opposite sentiment. "Certainly private school students should have access to certain benefits of the public education system." After all, these families reason, they pay taxes to fund the public school system, whether or not they send their children to public schools.

The United States Supreme Court has ruled on a specific case that bears upon the private versus public school debate. Reversing a 1985 precedent by a narrow 5-4 vote, the Court ruled that public school teachers could enter parochial schools to teach remedial classes to disadvantaged children without violating the so-called separation of church and state.

Instead of dealing with broad philosophical questions of church and state, the Supreme Court looked at the specific situation where New York City and a group of parents wanted to send public school teachers into parochial schools to provide remedial instruction. According to the 1965 Elementary and Secondary Education Act, public monies may be spent on remedial education and counseling services to needy students, regardless of what type of school they attend. Yet in 1985, the Supreme Court decided that public school teachers could not teach in parochial schools but must instead offer remedial classes in a nonreligious setting. The Court had found that using government funds in this way in a parochial school setting violated the United States Constitution by "advancing religion."

Due to significant changes in how the current Supreme Court views Establishment Clause cases, the justices moved away from the presumption that the mere presence of public school employees assigned to parochial school grounds would constitute a symbolic union between government and religion. The Court indicated that the actual location of the instruction no longer served as a litmus test to determine if the program was constitutional.

With this ruling, the High Court reaffirmed its belief that the government could directly aid education in private, even religious, schools. The program at hand was found valid because the government offered to provide supplemental, remedial education to disadvantaged children regardless of their religious affiliation or school of choice.

In this case, there was no governmental indoctrination, no religious litmus test, and no excessive governmental interference.

Basically, there was no problem. Parents of public school students didn't stand up and cheer, but they should have, because when the government agrees to use tax dollars to pay for remedial instruction for disadvantaged children, no one loses. Public school students don't lose. We all win when children who need special help get what they need to succeed in learning. And learning, after all, is the goal of public education, isn't it?

THE POINT IS . . .

There's a book being handed out in public schools that's causing quite a stir. The book is filled with stories of love and romance. Its pages are full of tales of hatred and violence. It isn't a new book. In fact, the book is very old. It is—the Bible. But are Bibles really allowed to be handed out in public schools? In a word, YES. In fact, private individuals and groups may distribute Bibles to public school students. But it is important how and where they do it.

In a recent decision by the Fifth Circuit Court of Appeals, the court ruled that Bibles left in a box in a public school lobby do not violate the Establishment Clause. This means that the government does not establish a religion by allowing this type of Bible distribution. It is important to note that, in this case, no public funds were used to distribute the Bibles. Also, students had the opportunity to voluntarily take the Bibles from a box in the school lobby. Given these circumstances, the court ruled that the mere presence of the Bibles didn't raise Establishment Clause concerns.

The point of law is that private individuals or groups are free to distribute Bibles in public schools as long as the Bibles are available on a voluntary basis and no tax dollars are involved.

CARING FOR
SEVEN

As a lawyer and head of a legal organization that handles many pro-life, human rights, and religious discrimination cases, a day at the office can sometimes be a little discouraging. Since we offer assistance to people who have been persecuted or oppressed for their beliefs, we receive much more bad news than good news as people call and write to us about the trials they are facing.

And when I take a moment from thinking about cases, the daily papers don't provide much of a diversion. Lately, it seems there have been a flurry of infanticides—from a mother who shot herself in the stomach to kill her own baby, to the young woman who was caught in a hospital shutting off the air supply to her two-month-old daughter.

But November 1997 brought us an exception, as the story of the septuplets in Iowa unfolded. In a time where the papers seem to be full of stories of mothers who give birth in the bathroom and leave their children to die, Bobbi and Kenny McCaughey are a refreshing exception. When they discovered that Bobbi was pregnant with seven babies, the doctors suggested that a few of the children be aborted to increase the chance of the others surviving. But the couple, both Christians, refused because they believe their children are gifts from God.

In the weeks that followed, the McCaugheys did everything they could to protect their unborn babies. Bobbi spent twenty-two weeks confined to her bed before the babies were born by Cesarean section. And in the years ahead, the family may well face continued medical problems, not to mention the challenge of raising seven children the same age. Yet in the face of these challenges, the McCaugheys chose to give their children the best gift of all—life.

I remember another example of courage—a young man, seventeen years old, who discovered that his girlfriend was pregnant. Desperate to save the life of his child, the young father was forced to get a court injunction to stop his baby from being aborted. During the thirty-six-hour-delay, the mother changed her mind and decided to have the child after all.

In a world full of deadbeat dads and abusive husbands, it would have been a lot easier for the boy to just walk away from the situation. But he didn't. And somewhere there is a little boy or girl who lives because the father cared enough about his child to take action.

In sharing these stories, I am reminded of the selflessness of another young, unwed mother and her fiancé—who knew that he was not the father of the child that she carried. Mary and Joseph lived in a tightly-knit community and faced the possibility of shame and stigma that would follow them all their lives.

Yet in the face of all this, Mary chose to face the whispers and misunderstandings when she willingly accepted the message of the angel. Joseph had the courage to carry through with a marriage, even though he would raise a child who was not his own.

In this age of the easy disposal of life, we must do what we can to help others choose life over death, whether it is by working at crisis pregnancy centers, in our churches or workplaces, or even in our own homes and relationships.

THE POINT IS . . .

You park next to a car with a bumper sticker that says, "Pro-child, pro-choice." Do you: A. Shake your head in disgust, silently wondering how someone could be so misled? B. Shake your fist in anger, loudly screaming, "It's a child, not a choice"? or C. Look for common ground, creating opportunities to discuss your pro-life position? Hopefully, you picked C.

All too often, we who are pro-life see those who are pro-choice as our enemies. We hate them. We judge them. And most of all, we alienate them. We fail to find common ground. A woman named Frederica Mathewes-Green, a pro-lifer who used to be pro-choice, criticizes the pro-life movement for these failures. To her critique, she adds some good advice that, I believe, could transform the pro-life movement. Her advice is that we view pregnant women and their unborn children as naturally linked pairs. Don't make them enemies. Second, figure out and meet the needs of pregnant women. Finally, help prevent unwanted pregnancies by encouraging responsible sexual behavior. Do research, give talks, and teach abstinence.

The point is that we must stop hating those who are pro-choice. We must rid ourselves of anger toward women seeking abortions. They are not the enemy. In fact, they are the very ones we should be loving—reaching out to—communicating with—finding common ground.

ZERO TOLERANCE POLICY VIOLATES STUDENTS' CONSTITUTIONAL RIGHTS

School administrators have a lot to deal with these days. Rather than rebuking children for chewing gum or running in the hall, they're forced to wage an unending battle against illegal drugs and students with guns. And in order to make any kind of difference, they need to have no-nonsense rules with strict application. The trouble is, some of the policies hurt those who are trying to help.

For example, when seven junior high students in Indiana were caught smoking marijuana at a basketball game, the school's no-drug, zero tolerance policy kicked in and the students found themselves kicked out of school. They knew the rule. They defied it. They took a fair punishment.

Several years later, though, Rob, an eighth grader at the same school, heard a friend threaten to commit suicide by overdosing on diet pills. Concerned, he took the pills away from her and reported the incident to his teacher. Under the zero tolerance policy, the school expelled Rob for the rest of the semester. The reason? He put the bottle of pills in his locker while he sought help for his friend.

It seems to me there are a lot of differences between the students using marijuana and one who tries to prevent a friend from

attempting suicide. Yet with some zero tolerance policies, there
is no room for discerning the difference. And kids like Rob end
up as victims—kicked out of the classroom with their reputations
tarnished.

On the one hand, there's no doubt that administrators have
a lot to contend with. According to a study by the University of
Michigan and the Department of Health and Human Services,
teen drug use has more than doubled since 1992. More than half
of all graduating high-school seniors state they have been
involved with illegal drugs. More than one-third of seniors used
marijuana within the past year. With statistics like that, no wonder some schools have started to play hardball.

On the other hand, though, some zero tolerance policies fly in
the face of common sense—and some are actually unconstitutional.

First, schools have banned items that are not illegal drugs; for
example, in Virginia two students were recently suspended for
playing with an Alka-Seltzer tablet in the cafeteria. Another child
was suspended one day for having a Certs breath mint.

Second, a student has a right to public education—and he
cannot be deprived of this without "due process of law" (Fifth
Amendment). That means he has the right to a fair trial. And during the fair trial, he should be given an opportunity to defend
himself. His motivations should be taken into consideration. As
in the courtroom, laws are never completely "one-size-fits-all,"
and mitigating circumstances need to be considered.

(Some states with zero tolerance policies have authorized the
local Board of Education to make exceptions to the rule case-by-
case. This is a step in the right direction. It also allows schools
and parents to work together, making justifiable decisions.)

Third, according to the Eighth Amendment, the punishment
should fit the crime. A marijuana smoker should have more
severe consequences than a Certs-popper. And expelling a boy for
preventing a potential suicide seems to fall into the category of
"cruel and unusual punishment."

In conclusion, in spite of real problems with drug use in public schools, we cannot implement policies that violate the constitutional rights of American students. We need reasonable rules, just trials, and fair punishments. Real crimes need real punishments, but little children with breath mints just don't fall into this category.

THE POINT IS . . .

Before high-school students in Arlington, Texas, head to their prom, they'd better be sure they've checked their breath. If some school board members have their way, students must pass a Breathalyzer test to gain admittance to the prom. No matter how fresh their breath smells, if alcohol is detected, they'll have to check out from the prom. Some parents welcome the alcohol test and hope it will deter students from drinking before the prom. Yet other parents—as well as students— regard the breath test as a deterrent to personal freedom and a violation of their rights. The school board will also vote on a "zero tolerance" drug policy. Under such a policy, any student found using alcohol or drugs on or off school property would be banned from all extracurricular activities.

The point of law is that the Fourth Amendment protects American citizens from unwarranted searches and seizures. This is one of the vital freedoms that our forefathers fought for and died to protect. Sadly, far too many Americans are willing to hand over their freedoms—and those of their children—if they think their safety is involved.

ON *JURASSIC PARK* AND PUBLIC SCHOOLS

It may seem odd at first, but the Tyrannosaurus Rex in *Jurassic Park* reminds me a little of the public school system—they're both large, semi-uncontrollable consumers who occasionally terrify children. But the similarities end there. Dinosaurs apparently died out when the world refused to support them any longer. However, public schools keep right on kicking, even in the face of growing controversy.

I'm referring to the continuing debate over vouchers and school choice. Should the government pass on educational funds to parents, allowing them to choose the schools their children attend? Or should they continue to pour all funding into the public school system?

The voucher idea appears to be growing in favor—55 percent of parents support the idea, according to one 1997 survey. And educational statistics provide ample fuel for the fire. For example, the *Washington Post* reported that only about 40 percent of students in urban public schools (tested in fourth and eighth grade) were attaining basic skills in reading, math, and science. Add to that the fact that many children who attend inner-city schools are poor minorities who can't afford to move to neighborhoods with better public schools. All told, you will find some good reasons for a school-choice voucher program, especially for low-income, inner-city families.

On the other hand, some educational leaders respond the same as Bob Chase, the president of the National Education Association, who remarked recently that a voucher program would just drain the public schools of resources, "somewhat like a low-grade virus." Educators fear losing money, parental involvement, and brighter students to private schools. They believe a voucher program would cause the further deterioration of the public system, and they may be right.

Instead of skimming off the "cream of the crop" and struggling with the rest, the alternative may be just to start over. The American public has been pouring funding into the public school system for decades, without much measurable result. While some schools are better than others, the system as a whole doesn't seem to serve our children as well as it should.

But if we scrap the whole system and start over, what should be done differently? On the one hand, smaller class sizes or good tutoring personnel can make a big difference. On the other hand, Catholic high schools have a higher percentage of students who finish high school and enroll in college—and they do it with relatively large class sizes and low teacher salaries. It seems that class size, finances, good teachers, self-discipline, parental involvement, and high educational standards all play a role—but none of these factors is the "whole answer" since different children bloom in different environments. Consequently, it seems that American children need options. Whether the schools are public or private, large or small, they should be versatile enough to accommodate and challenge every child.

Obviously, a single public or private school usually cannot provide this diversity. However, if students are offered a selection of specialized schools (public, private, or both), along with funding to choose the program that works best for them, this could more likely be attained. After all, that is exactly how our colleges function. Federal money (through Pell grants, etc.) is distributed to students who need it. In turn, those students gravitate toward the schools that serve them best—local community colleges, specialized training programs, Ivy League institutions, or religious colleges.

Perhaps the public school system, as it currently exists, needs to give way to a new system that offers more choice and more challenges to more students.

THE POINT IS . . .

Have you ever signed a contract? Perhaps it was a real estate contract with a licensed agent. Or maybe you signed a partnership agreement with a business associate. Chances are, you've never signed a parental contract with your local public school. But that's exactly what parents in Virginia were asked to sign: a contract in which parents agreed to "cooperate" with school officials in managing their children. Anyone who failed to sign the agreement risked a $50 fine and possible court action.

Well, our phones started ringing just as soon as parents began receiving their contracts to sign. On behalf of the 100 families in over thirty-five school districts who contacted The Rutherford Institute for help, we filed a lawsuit challenging the contract. In response, Virginia's General Assembly voted unanimously to revise their state law, eliminating both the $50 fine and the contract. Under the new law, parents will receive a note acknowledging their constitutional rights and will be asked to verify that they've received a copy of the school's conduct code.

A government official or organization, such as a public school, can never replace the role of parents. But if there is a vacuum of leadership and responsibility, history tells us that the government, or someone else, will assume the opportunity to influence our children. Parents, it's your job to make sure there's no vacuum of leadership—no window of opportunity to be seized from you or your children.

NOTHING NEW UNDER THE SUN— GENERATION X

They've been called "a generation without a conscience," "baby busters" or just "Generation X." But regardless of the title, the generation under examination includes my children, their friends, and many members of my staff—including lawyers, writers, and graphic artists. Consequently, it is always interesting to read what researchers are generalizing about these "twentysomethings."

For years, these young people faced the stigma of being aimless, depressed, nihilistic, and unmotivated. It's true that X-ers grew up in a violent society and a rapidly changing world. Many found themselves on their own, while their parents buried themselves in more-than-full-time jobs. They watched technology change, as e-mail and computer chat rooms replaced neighborhood interaction. And on top of that, if their parents were around, they expected the X-ers to "head for the top," whether in grade school or in life.

Interestingly, though, even with a life of upheaval and pressure to succeed, X-ers don't seem to be finding much satisfaction in what they have attained. Many are better off financially at an earlier age than their parents or grandparents, but they're finding that this doesn't satisfy.

Instead of settling for hedonism or wealth, it seems many X-ers simply desire the intimacy that people have always longed for. Chip Walker, the director of global marketing for Phillips (the electronics maker), summed it up well. "You get constant change coming at you," he said, "and the reaction is to head to the things of comfort—family, religion, marriage, kids."

And heading for security they seem to be. When it comes to matters of faith, one 1997 survey reported that one-fourth of the X-ers had a "great deal of confidence in organized religion," and 40 percent felt it was important to attend church regularly. And 47 percent believed that church teaching played an important part in their decision-making. All these statistics were slightly higher than for their parents—the baby boomers.

In addition, it appears that promiscuity, careerism, and abortion are in less favor than a few years ago—because many teens and young adults have changed their views. "What is eliciting such a change is a matter of speculation," wrote Frederica Mathewes-Green, a syndicated columnist and commentator for National Public Radio. "Perhaps it's the undeniable evidence of past failure, the dawning of reality, a deeper understanding of what really satisfies in life, or a renewed respect for the guidelines offered by biology."

Instead of substituting promiscuity for family relationships, X-ers are getting married younger. While the average age of brides in 1990 was twenty-seven, today it is twenty-four. Even large home industries are hurrying to adjust to the new homemaker market. For example, Williams-Sonoma, a culinary store, has begun offering items such as stainless-steel toasters in trendy colors like green, yellow, and orange. According to *Time* (November 10, 1997), the Gen X-ers are becoming "Gen Nesters."

In any case, faith and family remain the things of comfort. In the long run, that basically does not change. In spite of the boomers' attempts (or perhaps because of them) to find comfort in free love or (later) in financial success, the X-ers are asking for what people have wanted for centuries—a home where they feel secure, relationships where they feel loved, and perhaps even the security of a religious faith.

A generation goes and a generation comes. . . . Is there anything of which one might say, "See this, it is new"?

THE POINT IS . . .

It's Sunday morning or Wednesday night in America. Your children grumble, but you pack them off to church anyway. You know they need the instruction and spiritual guidance, even if they complain about having to be so holy. But at least they're going to church—unlike most other children in our torn and fractured world.

A new survey by the Roper Group found that, in the United Kingdom, only 14 percent of children attend church once a week. In Germany, the numbers are even lower. In the birthplace of the Protestant Reformation, only 11 percent of children attend religious services. And just 8 percent of French children go to church. The disturbing trend spirals downward even further in China and Japan.

The United States, however, stands apart from the crowd. The Roper survey discovered that 55 percent of American children aged seven to twelve attend religious services once a week—a higher percentage than England, Germany, and France combined!

The point is, as religion declines in other nations, we must fight to keep it a vital part of our culture. We cannot stand by and let the status quo set the standards for how we worship.

THE
INTERNATIONAL VIEW

TOLERATING ABUSE

For the avid moviegoer, *Seven Years in Tibet* probably wasn't the hit release of 1997. But for human rights advocates, the movie added a new dimension to the October visit of the Chinese president to the United States. At least some people who previously knew nothing about Tibet now partly understand why protesters dogged the steps of President Jiang Zemin.

President Jiang met with President Clinton; they "engaged" and disengaged, and Jiang went home again. But, far from being an isolated event, Jiang's visit simply highlighted an issue that continues to brew—should every person in the world be treated with the same dignity? Are there universal human rights that all governments should respect?

On December 10, 1997, the United Nations celebrated the forty-ninth anniversary of its Universal Declaration of Human Rights—a small document that boldly claims that every individual has a right to life, to liberty, to freedom of religion, and that people should not be subjected to torture, to slavery, or to forced marriages. But some member nations have taken issue with this, claiming that cultural rights and social rights are just as important as individual rights. To put it simply, they don't believe there *are* universal human rights.

Sadly, under the banner of "tolerance," Americans may let them get away with it. Secretary of State Madeleine Albright summed up this reluctance to confront human rights violations head-on when she remarked, "Even the most patriotic among us must admit that neither morality nor respect for human rights were invented—nor are they perfectly practiced—here."

She's partly right. After more than fifteen years of fighting religious discrimination in the courts, I agree that our justice system is imperfect. But that is simply a challenge to improve our own country, not an indication that our beliefs are fundamentally wrong. Nor is it evidence that we should blind our eyes to the problems in other nations. The real question is whether individuals have certain rights that should be protected, no matter where they live or who is in power.

Perhaps the issue becomes clearer as we consider just what we are asked to tolerate. Should we tolerate Pakistan, where the Taliban Islamic movement has closed schools for girls and banned women from holding jobs in the workplace? Should we tolerate wife beating in Kenya, forced marriages of minors in Iraq, forced abortion and the persecution of religious believers in China? Should we overlook the fact that several Catholic priests have been beheaded in India because they aided "untouchables" while, in some villages, young people who marry without permission are killed by their own families?

It's one thing to accept the idea of cultural rights superseding individual rights. It's another thing to live in a country where this is the case.

In the past, Americans have been leading champions in the arena of human rights—taking action in countries from Nazi Germany to South Africa to Bosnia, speaking out against abuses. But if we bow to the call for "tolerance" or remain silent until we're perfect, we do ourselves and the rest of the world a great injustice.

It's a tricky question of if, when, and where to become involved, but we can't simply walk away from it as easily as we walk away from *Seven Years in Tibet*. And we can't just give up the battle by accepting the lie that injustice isn't really injustice as long as it happens to somebody else.

THE POINT IS . . .

Blasphemy. God takes this sin very seriously. But what does blasphemy really mean? Basically, it means defaming the name of God. In America, people commit blasphemy every day, with no legal penalty. But this is not so in Pakistan. In the country of Pakistan, demeaning Allah carries with it the penalty of death. You see, back in 1991, the court of Islamic law made death by hanging the punishment for blasphemy. And as a result, Muslim zealots have targeted Christians and other non-Muslim religious believers for alleged blasphemous acts. Many Christians have been killed due to false allegations. And many more have been thrown into prison.

In fact, when a Catholic bishop staged a protest against Pakistan's strict blasphemy laws, he and four others were arrested and imprisoned. And though a judge has released the protesters, their pending trial could land them back in jail.

The point is that this Islamic law has led to acts of violence against Catholic and Protestant believers in Pakistan. In an attempt to protect the rights and lives of these non-Muslims, The Rutherford Institute contacted Pakistan's prime minister. We urged Prime Minister Bhutto to intervene on behalf of those who have protested the Islamic law. And we asked Bhutto to stop the bloodshed against Christians. This truly is injustice.

MORE NEWS FROM CHINA

When reports filtered out of China alleging that some individuals may be eating aborted children, it seemed time for the human rights abuses to end. Yet the long series of abuses continues to grow. If we, those who fight for freedom and the sanctity of life, do not start paying attention and taking action, an entire nation of people will be lost to the tyranny of its government.

The latest tales of abuse emerged when Human Rights Watch/Asia, a monitoring group based in New York, published a 331-page report on the state of children in Chinese orphanages. The group examined a Shanghai orphanage from the late 1980s to the early 1990s and documented the high death rate among the children admitted. The report alleges that the orphanage staff uses starvation as a means of controlling the population and then falsifies records, attributing the deaths to "congenital malformation of the brain."

The report, though largely the testimony of one woman who worked from 1988 to 1993 in the orphanage known as the Shanghai Children's Welfare Institute, is corroborated by photographs of the dying children taken by a former Chinese orphan, Ai Ming. One picture shows eleven-year-old Jian Xun ten days before he died of malnutrition, every bone in his body accentuated and his wrists tied to the bed on which he lies.

The Chinese State Council denies the truth of these reports.

But this latest is the fourth account to be published on child abuse in China's orphanages. And it is replete with details and quotes from many Chinese insiders such as officials from the Civil Affairs Ministry and lawyers from the Shanghai General Labor Union who verify the appalling conditions in the orphanages. The graduate medical student working in Shanghai's orphanage, Zhang Shuyan, included in the Human Rights Watch report medical records that showed that, over a thirteen-month period, 153 children died.

Zhang claims that children were frequently given sleeping pills when hungry and that those who complained or misbehaved were labeled mentally ill. From 1988 to 1993, the orphanage cited "congenital maldevelopment of the brain," "malnutrition," mental illness, and cerebral palsy as the leading causes of death.

Many of the victims of the orphanage are female babies who are not valued as much as male offspring due to the one-child policy in China. Others are orphans who may have slight physical disabilities but are mentally sound.

When will this list of human atrocities finally end? How many more abuses of the Chinese government must be exposed before the United States and its people take action? The Chinese people will not be the ones to lead the uprising against a government that silences its people through fear.

China expert Steven Mosher emphasizes the trouble he has encountered as a researcher trying to turn the private tragedies he hears into public outcries. "The Chinese government governs by force. Even in this country, the Chinese still do not feel that they are beyond the reach of the Beijing regime," which often threatens "their relatives in China."

It is time we acted upon what we know about China's human rights abuses. If we remain silent, then we are only condoning China's actions. How many products do we buy each day that carry the label "Made in China"? How many businesses have expanded into China in recent years?

We should not be supporting a nation that tortures its prisoners, forcibly aborts its babies, and starves its orphans. Our president must take a stand against the human rights abuses in China, not as an international leader but as another human being defending the human race.

We are all created equal before God, and we should consider it our moral responsibility to defend human life wherever it is being assaulted.

THE POINT IS . . .

Have you gone shopping yet this week? If so, how many products did you purchase that carry the label, "Made in China"? Well, the next time you grab an item off the shelves and head to the checkout counter, be sure to look for that little gold-colored label that says, "Made in China." And think for a moment what you're supporting: a long line of human rights abuses including mandatory abortions, fetal consumption, and orphan starvation.

The point is that we will be held accountable for how we respond to the knowledge we have. We know of human rights abuses in China. Now, I ask you, how are you responding to this knowledge? If we who are fighting for religious freedom and the sanctity of human life do not start paying attention and taking action, an entire nation will be lost to the tyranny of its government.

RUSSIA'S SEARCH FOR MEANING: IMPLICATIONS FOR RELIGIOUS LIBERTY

Minority religions in the newly "democratic" Russia are holding their collective breath right now as the fallout begins from a new law that threatens to cut them off from expressing their religious beliefs. Here in the United States it may seem that this law is of no relevance to us. But as John Donne so aptly pointed out, we are not alone on an island; what affects one affects us all. In other words, loss of religious liberty anywhere is a loss for religious liberty everywhere.

The law targets so-called cults and was pushed by the heavily entrenched Orthodox Church. Religions with less than a fifteen-year presence in Russia will see missionary activity restricted, in addition to facing strict controls on schools and seminaries and their right to distribute literature. Since the former Soviet Union was officially atheist and state-sanctioned religious activity was rare, many religious groups do not meet the fifteen-year requirement.

But this law really points to a larger struggle in the new Russia—as well as in Eastern Europe as a whole—that is, the struggle to deal with fundamental questions about life and society that those of us in the West have been dealing with for several centuries.

The totalitarian impulse still runs strong beneath the surface of former Communist countries. Freedom isn't a heritage, but a newly arrived phenomenon that is viewed with suspicion in many sectors of Eastern European society. Nonconformity to the establishment is still considered dangerous.

Yet even more insidious than this strong instinct to control expression through the state is the belief that maybe freedom as envisioned and implemented by the West is not for Russia or Eastern Europe. It's the belief that Western liberties are danger-ous; that these so-called freedoms contribute to a degenerate youth and a crime-ridden society. The Orthodox Church appar-ently played on these fears by pointing to the danger of cults. One thinks of those such as the Aum Supreme Truth in Japan that terrorized Tokyo subway passengers with poison gas. Russia responded to this fear of faceless "cults" by curtailing the rights of all minority religions, simply because of their minority status.

Russia and her peers in Eastern Europe must remember, how-ever, that true freedom brings with it some initial chaos—in addi-tion to every free society's ongoing dialogoue ver the definitions of true freedom.

America did not come by her heritage of liberty for all eas-ily. In fact, it is an ongoing struggle. Approximately 100 years after the Declaration of Independence, America fought another bitter revolution against an enemy within. The American Civil War threatened to rip the country apart. And it started because two large, powerful factions disagreed on the parameters of free-dom. The struggle continues today, in what the American media has labeled the "Culture Wars."

True freedom, then, often requires the blood, sweat, and tears of those who would possess her. Russia and Eastern Europe must not give up on their democratic experiment. To use a biblical analogy, the road to totalitarianism may be broad, but in the end it leads to destruction. Narrow is the way to freedom, however, and our prayer is that Russia and her fellow Eastern European countries be among those that find it.

THE POINT IS . . .

In order to expand your view of religious discrimination by opening your eyes to persecution around the world, I'd like to tell you about three countries where it's not only politically incorrect to be a Christian, it is downright dangerous. The countries are Sudan, China, and Pakistan.

Here's what's happening: In Sudan, individuals who don't accept the government religion are denied food and medicine. Reports indicate that Christians have been crucified, tortured, and burned alive. In China, "more Christians are imprisoned for their faith than in any other country in the world." House churches are targeted, raided, and their leaders imprisoned or "reeducated." In Pakistan, a twelve-year-old was sentenced to death under a blasphemy law that declared speaking out against Mohammed a crime punishable by death. According to World Missions Digest, *more people around the world have been martyred for their Christian faith in this century than in the previous nineteen centuries combined.*

CONCLUSION

BELIEVERS VS. THE STATE

The Christian believer who truly lives his or her faith is a true minority in America. And those who are willing to stand up for their faith are finding themselves increasingly at odds with the goals of modern culture and the state. The issue today is no longer the church versus the state. It is, instead, the *religious believer versus the state.*

For example, in cases where a child writes "I Love Jesus" on her valentine and her public school teacher says the valentine must be censored because of the "separation of church and state," the question is: where is the church? There is no church involved but simply a lone religious child versus the state.

It is the *individual*, the solitary person deeply committed to his or her religious views, who is suffering the loss of religious liberty in America. Nadine Strossen, president of the ACLU, acknowledges this fact. "I think we have a secular society in which people who have deeply held religious beliefs of any kind are looked at with some suspicion," she observes. "For example, if somebody had a religious view against abortion, I think it's the religion that's looked at with special suspicion rather than the same belief but based on a secular reason."

Examples of this public animosity toward religion are legion. To cite just a few:

In February 1997, The Rutherford Institute intervened on

behalf of a public school girl who was prohibited from singing a song in her school's talent show because it contained the name "Jesus."

Also in February, The Rutherford Institute thwarted the ACLU's attempt to prohibit a West Virginia public school from making Bibles available in school lobbies for students to take voluntarily.

In April, a federal appeals court ruled that a minister who was dismissed from his post on San Francisco's Human Rights Commission because he refused to disavow biblical passages on homosexuality had no legal recourse against the city.

These cases represent the *privatization* of religion in America. Although most Americans will not yet challenge the *right* to be religious, increasing numbers of Americans appear to believe that religion should be *exercised* only in private. As Supreme Court Justice Antonin Scalia has noted, "Church and state would not be such a difficult subject if religion were, as the Court apparently thinks it to be, some purely personal avocation that can be indulged entirely in secret, *like pornography, in the privacy of one's own room.*"

Yet Christians hold a major responsibility for the removal of religion from public life. A significant factor in this state of affairs has been the dwindling influence of Christianity that has permitted secular thought to dominate the culture. The noted British theologian H. G. Wood notes: "Somehow the whole bottom has fallen out of our civilization, and a change came over the world, which if unchecked will transform it for generations. It is the death, or deathlike swoon, of Christianity."

To prevent this, it will require a refocusing on the Christian faith. If those who call themselves Christian believers do not once again begin to meet the real human needs of people in speaking God's truth, the future, as Wood observes, looks dim indeed.

CHRISTIANS IN A TORN WORLD

Our world today is ravaged with crises, tragedies, and horrors. To cite a few:

In the Tiananmen Square massacre (June 3-4, 1989), hundreds, if not thousands, of Chinese students and other demonstrators were killed as the Communist government cracked down on pro-democracy speech.

In blasphemy and apostasy trials in Pakistan and Kuwait, Christians receive death sentences; one example of extreme religious intolerance is in the Middle East where the situation continues to be of concern.

In the April 1995 bombing of a federal building in Oklahoma City, 168 people were killed. It has been theorized that the bombing was an extremist response to the federal government's participation in the killing of over eighty people in April 1993 in Waco, Texas, at the Koresh Compound.

These crises and issues demand a clear Christian response. Indeed, the world desperately needs Christians who will engage every facet of life. "Good citizenship," as Charles Colson writes in his book *Kingdoms in Conflict* (1987), "requires both discernment and courage—discernment to assess soberly the issues and to know when duty calls one to obey or disobey, and courage, in the case of the latter, to take a stand."

All too often modern Christians portray Jesus Christ as a

meek, harmless friend to the world. Far from being passive or meek, however, Christ was both controversial and dogmatic. Jesus Christ was not "broad-minded" in the modern sense, nor was He multicultural. He was not prepared to accept as valid all views on every subject. Christ was not afraid to dissent from official or popular doctrines that He knew were wrong.

Jesus Christ took truth to the world and commanded His disciples to do likewise. He also told them that if they followed His example, they could expect rejection and persecution.

Modern Christians in the West, much like their counterparts in other areas of the world, face the very real potential of being driven from American public life. Once that is accomplished, Christianity will be excised from the basic foundations of the country, and oppression will result.

If we are to engage the culture and glorify God, we must be willing to be *the Christians Jesus Christ told us to be*. What does this mean?

First, it means that *we must be controversial*. We must understand that controversy flows from the collision of truth with falsehood. Controversy, however, should not result from the *manner* in which truth is presented but rather from the truth itself. In other words, in a confrontational situation, controversy should be the result of the *message*, not the messenger.

Second, *our Christian message must be comprehensive*; it should speak to *all* of life, not just to theological or so-called "religious" concerns. The comprehensive nature of the truth expressed by the apostles, especially Paul, must be restored if Christians are to be effective in preaching the Gospel.

Third, *Christians must engage in "cautious radicalism" and, if necessary, civil disobedience*. Peter's resistance in Acts 5 is a classic example of standing for religious principles against the illegitimate acts of the state. In response to the charges of preaching in Jesus' name, Peter replied: "We must obey God rather than men." The apostles were then beaten and commanded not to teach about Christ.

However, as the Bible notes, "Daily in the temple, and in every house they ceased not to teach and preach Jesus Christ." Nothing could stop the apostles. They were too intent on turning the world upside down for Christ. Their obedience in the face of persecution is the challenge for each Christian in today's torn world.